the Big Grill

the Big Grill

Paul Kirk

FRIEDMAN/FAIRFAX
PUBLISHERS

A QUINTET BOOK

This edition is published by Friedman/Fairfax
by arrangement with Quintet Publishing Limited
2003 Friedman/Fairfax Publishers

Please visit our website: http://www.metrobooks.com

Distributed by Sterling Publishing Company, Inc.
387 Park Avenue South
New York, NY 10016

Distributed in Canada by Sterling Publishing
Canadian Manda Group
One Atlantic Avenue, Suite 105
Toronto, Ontario, Canada M6K 3E7

Library of Congress Cataloging Data available upon request.

ISBN 1 58663 925 0

M 10 9 8 7 6 5 4 3 2 1

This book was designed and produced by
Quintet Publishing Limited
6 Blundell Steet
London N7 9BH

Photography Juliet Piddington
Food stylist Kathryn Hawkins
Art direction and Design Simon Daley
Editor Erin Connell

Managing Editor Diana Steedman
Creative Director Richard Dewing
Publisher Oliver Salzmann

Manufactured in Singapore by Universal Graphics
Printed in China by Leefung-Asco Printers Trading Ltd

Contents

BARBECUE BASICS

A short history of barbecuing

How barbecuing actually started is unknown. I would venture to guess that an unfortunate animal got caught in a volcanic eruption or fell into a fire pit, and a man came along and pulled it out, accidentally ending up with some of the hot flesh on his hands. He licked his hand, liked what he tasted and never looked back. That's only one theory – there are many others – but what is known is that people have been cooking over coals since the beginning of time. Ancient barbecue pits have been unearthed during archeological digs in China and, more recently, in Spain, where a 150,000-year-old pit was unearthed. The existence of fire pits to cook meats has been dated as far back as 2500 BC. The writings of Homer suggest that the Greeks were preparing oxen, sheep, and swine in an open grill or fire pit long before the birth of Christ. Homer tells us that Achilles prepared a meal for Ajax, Odysseus, and Phoenix in which a sheep, a goat, and a pig were butchered and salted, then grilled over live coals. But how did we get the name barbecue? Early Spanish explorers came to the New World and found the Native Americans cooking their meat on sticks and on grills, which they called *barbacoa* – which was translated to the word barbecue that we use today.

A world of barbecues

Barbecue as we know it today has enjoyed a boom in popularity during the last several decades, not only in the United States, Australia and Europe, but all over the globe. The oldest cooking method known is still being practiced and with delicious results. Here is a brief tour of barbecuing and grilling around the world.

In South Korea, you may enjoy *bulgogi* – thin strips of beef marinated in soy sauce, rice wine, and seasonings. The meat and accompaniments are brought to you to cook the meal yourself over a grill in the center of the table. The grill is shaped like a hubcap, has a brass grill-top, and is fueled with bamboo charcoal. You cook the meat to the desired doneness, wrap it in a green leaf lettuce or sesame leaf, and top it with kimchee (a fiery hot sauce made with cabbage, garlic, and onions). It is truly delightful.

In Japan, there are many different grilling techniques. In restaurants, the customer cooks teriyaki chicken and beef kabobs over a grill set into the middle of the table. Shrimp, squid (calamari), and yakitori (marinated chicken and leeks on skewers) are often cooked outdoors on a Japanese barbecue or *hibachi*. People may go to yakitori stands, which are very basic affairs – perhaps six stools pushed against a counter that houses the *hibachi*. The succulent skewers are dipped in a sauce and then grilled to perfection, usually washed down with a cold beer. Okonomiyaki shops, which are very popular with students, involve cooking your own vegetable-filled pancake on a charcoal-fired hot plate in the center of the table.

A signature Indonesian grilled dish is *saté* – marinated cubes of meat, fish, or poultry threaded onto skewers and grilled over a hot fire. *Saté* is served with peanut and other sauces, using a recipe derived from the Arab spice traders.

The Thai people grill using bamboo- and coconut shell-charcoal. Their tangy and delicious marinades are based on lime juice, garlic, galangal, lemongrass, and hot peppers. Basic charcoal grills are set up on the pavement to cook kabobs, fish, and marinated chicken. The method is simple and the ingredients are often few, but the results are mind blowing.

In Brazil, restaurants serve whole joints of meat that have been grilled on large, sword-like skewers. The skewers are then brought to your table where a portion is carved off. Known as *churrasco*, it is both a great feast and a great spectacle.

Jerk is Jamaican barbecue, and is a cooking method, a national dish, and a way of life. Spicy and tasty, it is a blend of Scotch bonnet chile peppers, allspice, and lime juice or vinegar. Jamaican jerk has been traced back to the Arawak Indians, who are credited as one of the originators of barbecue.

The Argentinians grill in several ways. One way is by covering the ground with hot coals and staking a whole lamb or suckling pig into the ground, positioning it so it's angled towards the fire in order to cook slowly and succulently. The second way, which can be attributed to the Gauchos, is to grill small foods like sausages, mixed grill skewers, kidneys, and other organ meats.

The Australians are barbecue aficionados, and at public beaches you find large, open bar grills that are available for anyone to use, making them great places to hold cook-outs. There is an abundance of fresh fish and shellfish, and "surf and turf" (fish and meat dishes) is popularly eaten together.

Turkish skewered meat or fish is known as *shish kebab*, while the large rotating tower of meat slowly grilling in traditional Turkish restaurants is called *doner*. The Greeks enjoy spit-cooked lamb or skewered lamb as *souvlakia*, as well as minced pork and herbs served as *kebabs*.

Countries and cultures that prepare their own version of barbecue are almost too numerous to list: in North Africa and the Middle East, grilled food is called *meshwi*; in Mali, street vendors sell *kyinkyinga*, a type of kabob; in France, you would be served *brochettes*; and tilapia, grilled over a smoky charcoal fire, is a common sight in African streets.

These are just some of the countries where grilling is a way of life – breakfast, lunch, and dinner – all year round. As the motto of the Kansas City Barbecue Society goes, "Barbecue isn't just for breakfast anymore."

Getting fired up

Grilling is cooking food quickly over hot coals. Direct heat seals the food on the outside while the inside retains its tenderness and succulence. Barbecuing, traditionally, refers to cooking over indirect heat with the barbecue lid in place, as with a covered barbecue pit that allows heat to be conducted around the food, acting rather like an oven. This type of cooking is particularly suitable for whole chickens, legs of lamb, and large, meaty fish. However, this book goes along with popular conception and

makes little distinction between barbecuing and grilling. Where food should be covered by the lid to achieve an indirect heat this is indicated in the recipe.

Buying a barbecue or grill

A grill is any vessel that can hold a fire and withstand heat. It can be a simple hole in the ground or an elaborate ceramic structure offering you a complete "outdoor kitchen." When buying a barbecue or grill, you need to consider several factors, including the amount of money and space you have available, the type of fuel that you wish to use, how often you will use the grill and what you intend to cook on it. Outlined below are the most widely used types of fuel: charcoal, gas, and electric.

Charcoal grills For many, a charcoal grill is the only way to cook, and there is nothing that can be said or done to persuade them otherwise. Purists say that cooking over charcoal is the best way to achieve that delicious, smoky flavor in your food. They find that the building, stoking, and nurturing of the fire is part of the overall experience and tradition of barbecuing. Charcoal grills require more judgement and skill to be operated effectively than do gas or electric grills.

Kettle, covered, or hooded grills These three grills are similar, as they all feature a lid or cover. With the cover off, you can grill on an open rack; with the cover on, it is as though using a conventional oven because the heat circulates around the food. Either way, there is the additional bonus of imparting the aromas and flavors of open-fire cooking into your food. Kettle or hooded grills are particularly good for roasting because of their domed shape and the placement of air vents, and can add smoked flavors to foods if a handful of wood chips is added to the fire. Kettle barbecues are easy to store, easy to clean, and are versatile enough to cook a range of foods.

Hibachi Literally meaning "fire bowl," these traditional Japanese charcoal-burners are comprised of a shallow, cast iron bowl for the fire, along with a series of notches that allow the cooking racks to be raised and lowered. The heavier, cast iron models are more effective because the thicker metal distributes the heat better than in the lighter, steel versions. They are inexpensive and portable, making them the ideal choice for beach barbecues and picnics.

Pedestal or pillar grills These slender grills comprise a fire bowl set on a hollow tube that is stuffed with newspaper to help ignite the charcoal. When buying a pedestal grill, first consider its location in your garden, yard, or balcony because these grills need to have a very stable surface to stand on. They are easy to light, quick to reach cooking temperature, and the ventilation holes allow you to control the rate at which the coals burn.

Disposable grills These are small, cheap, and portable – perfect for picnics, the beach, or for barbecue novices who want to try grilling for the first time. They usually include a rack sitting over a foil tray of charcoal that has been impregnated with lighter fluid. They are easy to light, ready to use in about 15 minutes, and are perfectly suited to cooking smaller items such as sausages, burgers, kabobs, and vegetables.

Homemade grills A brick-built barbecue on your patio makes barbecuing part of your everyday life. There are commercial kits available containing fireboxes, grids, and racks that can be incorporated into a permanent or temporary brick structure. Homemade grills can be made from a range of materials, from a 55 gallon drum to a flowerpot. My father's first barbecue grill was made from 36 cinder blocks and two metal grates he purchased from the junkyard for a couple of dollars each. If you are seriously thinking about building your own barbecue, carefully consider its location. Avoid regularly used pathways, overhanging trees, children's play areas, and orientate the open side of the grill toward the prevailing breezes so that you can catch the drafts to keep the fire going.

Gas grills Gas grills are convenient and more easily controlled than charcoal grills, and the grill can be ready for use almost immediately. Available in a variety of sizes, from large trolleys to small, portable grills, the gas (propane or natural gas) heats the lava rocks or flavoring plates that cook the food. Gas

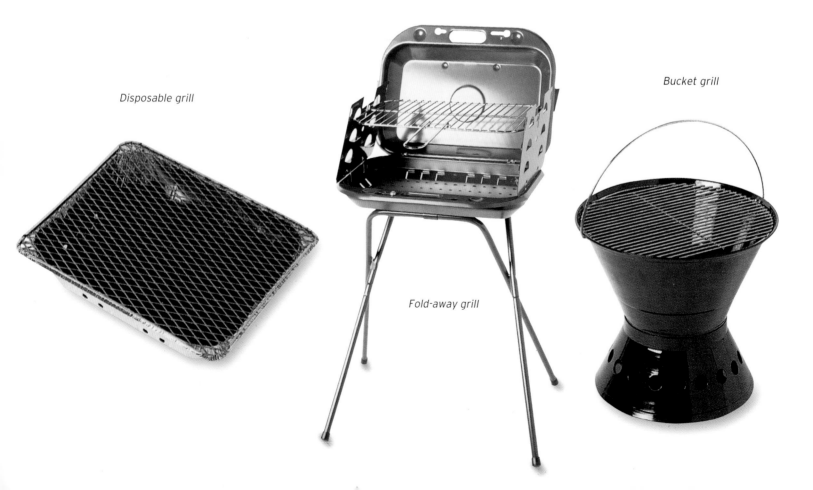

Disposable grill

Fold-away grill

Bucket grill

grill addicts argue that the taste achieved by gas barbecues matches that produced by charcoal grills in a fraction of the time. A large gas grill is ideal for large parties or for those who want to mingle with their guests without havin gto keep a constant eye on the fire! They are a good choice when there is the opportunity for frequent use, with small parties.

Wagon or trolley grills Fast, easy to use, and versatile, the trolley barbecue is an all-around grill, with some models featuring three or four burners, a wok burner, and a rotisserie. Often gas-powered, trolley barbecues can be expensive and require a lot of storage space because of their size. They are movable rather than portable, but are generally fuss-free and versatile enough to cook a range of foods.

Electric grills Available in a range of sizes, from the large trolley to the smaller, more portable versions, the electric grill offers the same advantages as the gas grill. Electric grills provide a good constant heat source but do not get as hot as charcoal. Another disadvantage of electric grills is that you

have to be close to a power source or have an extension cord long enough to reach the grill site. This may also involve taping down wires to ensure the safety of everyone in your party.

The right fuel

The success of a great barbecue is a great fire. Deciding on the best fuel-type for you will come with experimentation and experience. For minimum fuss, gas is likely to be your best choice. But if you enjoy the whole outdoor experience, then give charcoal a go. Whatever you choose, with a little practice and knowledge of technique, you will be cooking up a storm.

Lump or natural charcoal Made by burning hardwood without oxygen until all the impurities have been removed, the result is pure carbon – a black, glossy, lightweight product. Natural charcoal burns hotter and cleaner than charcoal

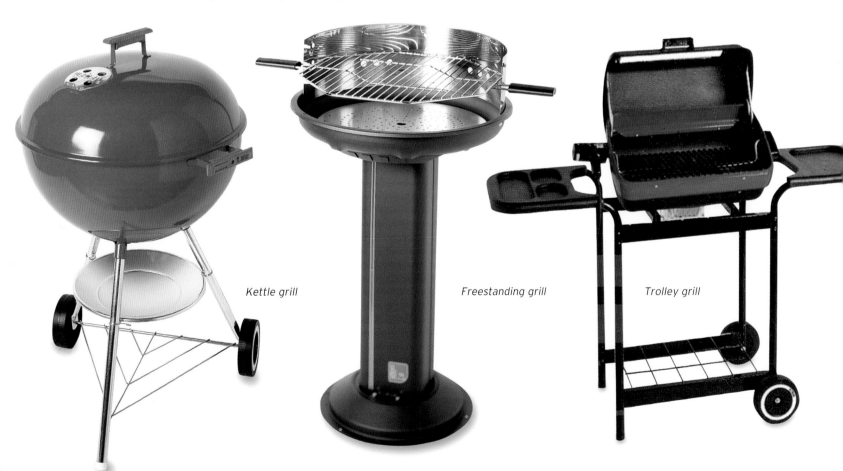

Kettle grill   *Freestanding grill*   *Trolley grill*

briquettes. Charcoal ignites quickly and burns fairly quickly for about 45 minutes, perfect for searing food while helping it retain its succulence.

Briquette charcoal Briquette charcoal, which is widely available, is made from compressed charcoal particles, and is often impregnated with chemicals to help it ignite more easily. Briquette charcoal provides a consistent and steady heat and tends to burn longer than natural charcoal. Briquettes are also available made from pecan shells, bamboo, and coconut husks, all of which burn hotter than domestic charcoal and impart their own unique flavors to the food.

Wood (logs, chunks, chips) Even with the wide availability of charcoal, wood-fire barbecuing is growing in popularity. Ensure that you know the source of the wood you burn and don't burn wood treated with chemicals, or soft wood such as pine which is full of resin. Use hardwood and fruit woods as below. If you are using charcoal, a handful of wood chips thrown on the hot coals will impart different flavors to your grill:

Hickory Pungent, smoky, bacon-like flavor

Oak Heavy smoke flavor

Apple Slightly sweet, but dense, fruity smoke flavor

Pecan Similar to oak but not as strong

Cherry Slightly sweet and fruity smoke flavor

Mesquite Strong, earthy flavors

Alder Delicate with a hint of sweetness

Maple Mild, smoky, sweet flavor.

Sure-fire tools and accessories

Before experiencing the thrill of the grill there are a few essential items that you need to be a flaming success.

Charcoal Chimney This is an inexpensive, cylindrical metal structure that can be set on the fire grate. Charcoal sits in the top section and crumpled newspaper in the bottom. It is handy for getting your fire going quickly and also helps to keep your fire supplied with hot coals. Start your extra coals in the chimney roughly 20 minutes before you need them.

Fire Starters Long stick matches are the obvious and safest choice, but there are many other methods of lighting up. Wax starters are long fibrous sticks soaked with paraffin or beeswax to aid the lighting process. I prefer to use the small, wax-like cubes specifically designed for lighting barbecues. Kindling (such as wood shavings or small twigs) and paper are useful additions to the charcoal fire if placed underneath the charcoal before lighting. The paper will often allow the fire to "catch" the briquettes. An electric fire starter is a wand that you plug into an electrical outlet and it glows red hot to start your charcoal. Never use any form of lighter fuel that has not been specifically *manufactured to light charcoal barbecues.* Never use petroleum-based firelighters even though they are safe to use, as they give off an odor that can taint the food.

Long-handled Cooking Tools These include tongs, fish slices for turning, basting brushes, forks and skewers for testing doneness, and spatulas for serving. Wooden-handled tools are best as they do not conduct heat as efficiently as metal.

Apron and Mitts Use a thick, nonflammable apron to protect your clothes, and heatproof mitts are essential.

Spritzing Bottles and Baking Soda A spritzing bottle of water and a carton of baking soda are useful items to douse the fire or control a flare-up. A second spritzing bottle containing basting liquid or apple juice is a good idea to keep the food moist and succulent.

Meat Thermometer If you are unsure of whether large joints of meat or whole chickens are cooked through, a meat thermometer measures the internal temperature.

Hinged Wire Grids or Grill Baskets These are available in various shapes and are designed to hold meat, fish, or vegetables. Using a basket makes turning the food easier, but be sure to wear your heatproof mitts when handling it.

Metal and Bamboo Skewers Flat skewers are the best because they stop food from slipping as you turn it on the grill. Bamboo skewers need to be soaked in cold water for 30 minutes prior to cooking to help prevent them from simply burning away on the barbecue. They will still char, but remain intact.

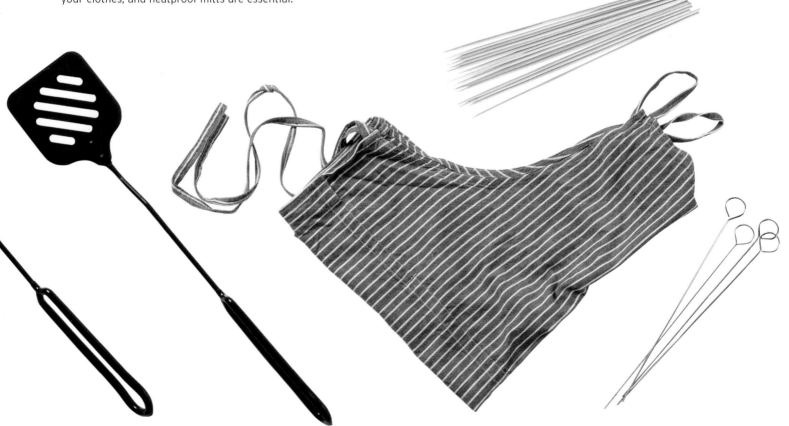

Lighting up

Your grill should be sited on a solid, level ground away from low trees. A smaller grill such as an *hibachi* can be raised from the ground but should be securely placed on a heat-resistant surface. In the event of sudden wet weather, never be tempted to try and grill indoors!

When lighting up, make sure you are dressed sensibly in a protective apron and mitts and that children and animals are a safe distance away. Make sure you have everything you need before you start, as a burning grill should never be left unattended. Never light up in a high wind, and always make sure that matches and lighter fuels are kept a safe distance away from the flame. In the event of a sudden flare-up, use your spritzer bottle of water or a handful of baking soda to douse the flames. In the (rare) event that a fire gets out of control, it is always useful to keep some sand handy to put out the flames.

Do not attempt to use charcoal in a gas grill. Check that the gas regulator is appropriate for your barbecue and that the connecting hoses and taps are in good working order. For electric grills, check the circuits and wires periodically and do not cook in wet weather.

From go to glow!

To light a charcoal grill, allow about 45 minutes before you want to start cooking. Remove the lid and open the vents wide. Spread charcoal briquettes, about two layers thick, across the base of the grill, piled into a neat heap in the center. Alternatively, put the fuel into a charcoal chimney and light. Leave the coals for 10 minutes or so until they glow red, then spread them back over the base in an even layer using long-handled tongs. Leave them for another 25 to 30 minutes to heat up, waiting until the charcoal is ash gray before starting to cook.

To light a gas grill, allow about 10 minutes preheating. Open the lid and turn on the burners. Close the lid and allow the heat to reach the desired cooking temperature. Refer to your manufacturer's instructions for this, but generally, a gas barbecue takes 10 to 15 minutes to heat up.

Grilling techniques are not difficult to master. Basically, to be successful, it is a matter of paying attention to what you are doing and keeping a close eye on the food.

THE HAND TEST

Now, use the "hand test" to judge the heat of your grill. Hold your hand palm side down over the coals. If you can hold your hand steadily over the heat for no more than 2 seconds, you can judge the fire hot. See below for a rough guide to other grill temperatures.

Hot	**2 seconds**
Medium-hot	**3 seconds**
Medium	**4 seconds**
Medium-low	**5 seconds**
Low	**6 or more seconds**

If your fire has become too hot, and you're running too fast, don't despair – just turn the food more frequently. Covering the grill, and/or closing the air vents, are other ways to lower the heat. For example, if you were cooking a pork tenderloin and the recipe suggests turning it every 5 to 7 minutes, but the heat is too high to wait that long without burning, turn it every 3 minutes instead. If the coals lose their heat, or you wish to prolong cooking time, add fresh coals around the hot coals; placing them on top will kill the heat.

All-season grilling

Many people enjoy year-round grilling, so your grill need not be sent into hibernation for the winter months. According to one leading survey, nearly half of all Americans grill all year long, which includes the winter months. I will grill 365 days a year if need be, and I have even cooked when the wind-chill factor made it feel like 21°F. However, there are significant differences between barbecuing in warm and cold weathers, not least to ensure heavier clothing is kept clear of the heat.

Cooking in cold weather will necessitate using 10 to 20 per cent more fuel, depending upon how windy and cold it is. It will also increase your cooking times, sometimes considerably. This is because heat dissipates more quickly from your barbecue in cold weather than it does in warmer weather. One solution is to insulate your grill using foil-backed insulation material. Securely wrap the foil around the bottom portion of the grill to insulate the firebox, and use a piece to help insulate the lid. Some barbecue manufacturers produce their own insulated covers to fit their designs, otherwise it could involve a bit of DIY!

Maintenance is important for your grill in the colder months. Before it gets cold, check your barbecue for efficiency, as grilling in cold weather puts more demands on your burners.

Keep your grill in a sheltered spot away from fences, low trees, and other flammable structures. If you cannot do this, then grilling outdoors on a windy evening is not recommended.

Allow sufficient time for the grill to warm up, over and above the usual heating times. The colder it is, the longer it will take for your grill to heat up. To keep the temperature up, add some raw coals or raw wood to your charcoal fire during the cooking process. The addition of raw fuels to the fire will keep the flames fed and the temperatures high. Never, however, add raw fuels to your gas barbecue.

Always keep your barbecue covered while cooking and try to avoid the temptation to lift the lid too often. Don't ignore your food, of course, but by limiting the amount of times the lid is removed, your cooking will take less time and your steaks will be succulent and delicious.

Red hot maintenance

Oil your grill racks regularly so that food does not stick. Keep your grill as free from grease as possible. To clean it, scrub the grill racks with a wire brush or spatula before and after cooking. Clean the ashes from your firebox when they have cooled and dispose of them in a metal trash can with a lid. Before storing the barbecue away for winter, use an oven cleaner to remove heavy, burnt-on deposits that have gathered on the grill grates.

Looking after your grill will make it last longer. At the end of the season, give all your tools a thorough cleaning, making sure to dry everything completely before storing it so that it doesn't rust. Try to store your barbecue away from the elements, or at the very least cover it properly with a waterproof covering.

MARINADES AND RUBS

Piri piri glaze

Piri piri is Portugal's favorite hot spicy sauce, and kicks this first section off with a powerful start!

3 hot red chiles, seeded and chopped finely
3 tbsp olive oil
3 tbsp packed brown sugar
1 tbsp white wine vinegar
2 cloves garlic, minced
1 tbsp tomato paste
$\frac{1}{2}$ cup water

1 Place all the ingredients in a small pan. Bring to a boil. Simmer over low heat until the glaze thickens.

2 Remove from the heat and let cool.

Makes $^3/_4$ cup

Barbecue mop

The proportion of vinegar may seem high in this recipe, but don't be put off by it, because it works well with fish, meat, or vegetables.

6 tbsp cider vinegar
3 tbsp water
$1^1/_2$ tbsp Worcestershire sauce
$1^1/_2$ tbsp vegetable oil
2 tsp sea salt
2 tsp freshly ground black pepper
$1^1/_2$ tsp cayenne pepper

Combine the ingredients in a medium bowl. Brush over the food to be grilled before cooking, and then frequently during cooking.

Makes $^1/_2$ cup

Orange honey glaze

Although this recipe is simple to make and uses only three ingredients, it packs a huge flavor punch.

6 tbsp honey
Zest and juice of 1 orange
2 tbsp mirin (sweet rice wine)

1 Place the ingredients in a small saucepan. Bring to a boil. Boil vigorously until reduced by half.

2 Remove from the heat and let cool. Use for brushing over meat during the last 10 minutes of grilling.

Makes $^1/_2$ cup

Opposite Piri piri glaze

Cajun dry rub

Chefs from New Orleans helped popularize Cajun cuisine, including spice rubs like the one here. You can buy premixed spice mixes in the supermarket, but nothing is ever as good as homemade.

2 tbsp hot paprika

1 tbsp dried thyme

1 tbsp ground cumin

1 tbsp garlic powder

1 tbsp onion powder

1 tsp freshly ground black pepper

1 tsp sea salt

1 tsp cayenne pepper

1 tsp ground marjoram

Combine the ingredients in a small bowl and mix well.

Makes ½ cup

How dow rub

An extraordinary name for a truly fiery rub to try on beef steaks or chicken.

1 tbsp dried mustard

3 tbsp hot paprika

1 tbsp onion powder

1 tbsp garlic powder

1 tbsp sea salt

1 tsp freshly ground black pepper

½ tsp bay leaf powder

Combine the ingredients in a small bowl and mix well.

Makes ½ cup

Mango butter

If mangoes are unavailable, substitute 4 ounces each of peaches and pineapple purée, and use as directed.

2 sticks unsalted butter, softened

8 oz fresh or jarred mango, peeled or drained and puréed

2 tsp lime juice

2 tbsp finely chopped fresh mint

1 tsp shredded nutmeg

Mash the softened butter with a fork and add the remaining ingredients. Wrap the mixture in plastic wrap and roll into the shape of a log. Refrigerate until needed.

Makes 1 cup

Above left Cajun dry rub **right** Mango butter

Green peppercorn butter

Pernod is a licorice-flavored liqueur from France. If you don't have it on hand, you may substitute any other licorice- or anise-flavored spirit.

1 tbsp green peppercorns preserved in brine, drained
1 stick unsalted butter, softened
3 shallots, chopped finely
1 tsp Pernod

1 Crush the peppercorns using a mortar and pestle.

2 Combine with the remaining ingredients in a small bowl.

3 Wrap in plastic wrap and roll into a log shape, about 1-inch in diameter. Refrigerate until needed.

Makes ½ cup

Butter, lemon, and herb marinade

To use, add to chicken, fish, or meat and marinate at room temperature for 1 hour or brush on while grilling. You can use dried herbs instead of fresh, but be sure to reduce the amount of herbs by half.

1 stick unsalted butter
Juice of 1 lemon
2 tbsp finely chopped, mixed fresh herbs, such as rosemary, thyme, and marjoram
4 cloves garlic, chopped
Freshly ground black pepper

1 Gently melt the butter in a saucepan. Add the remaining ingredients and mix well.

2 Cover and marinate food at room temperature for 1 hour, or brush on while grilling.

Makes about ½ cup

Honey and mustard marinade

If you like a little spice with your food, increase the dashes of cayenne pepper.

3 tbsp honey
1 tbsp dried mustard
3 tbsp olive oil
1 cup pineapple juice
Juice of 1 orange
2 tbsp tomato paste
Dash of cayenne pepper
Freshly ground black pepper to taste

1 Place the honey, mustard, oil, pineapple and orange juice, and tomato paste in a small saucepan and mix well. Bring to a boil and simmer for 15 minutes.

2 Stir in the cayenne and black pepper. Let cool before using.

Makes 1½ cups

Opposite Green peppercorn butter

Balsamic vinegar herb marinade

These days, a well-stocked kitchen includes a bottle of balsamic vinegar, so this marinade should be easy to throw together. This is especially good on grilled vegetables.

6 tbsp olive oil

2 tbsp balsamic vinegar

2 scallions (white and green parts), chopped finely

2 tbsp finely chopped parsley

1 tbsp finely chopped rosemary

1½ tsp finely chopped thyme

Sea salt and freshly ground black pepper to taste

Combine all the ingredients in a small bowl and mix well.

Makes about ½ cup

Chermoula

This marinade is a beautiful green color due to the abundance of fresh cilantro and parsley called for in the recipe.

1 bunch cilantro, chopped finely

1 bunch parsley, chopped finely

6 cloves garlic, minced

1 tbsp ground cumin

1 tsp ground coriander

1 tbsp paprika

¼ tsp cayenne pepper

Juice of 2 lemons

1¼ cups olive oil

Combine the dry ingredients in a large bowl and mix well. Add the lemon juice and oil and stir thoroughly.

Makes about 2 cups

Opposite Chermoula

Sweet-and-sour marinade

The exotic ingredients required here give a hint to its origins in Indonesia. Most Asian markets will carry the shrimp paste and a selection of soy sauces.

1 tbsp cumin seeds	8 tbsp hot water
1 tbsp coriander seeds	3 tbsp sweet soy sauce
3 tbsp peanut oil	3 tbsp lime juice
2 medium onions, peeled and chopped	¼ tsp chili powder
3 cloves garlic, peeled	Sea salt and freshly ground black pepper to taste
3 tbsp shrimp paste	

1 Roast the cumin and coriander seeds in a heavy skillet until they start to color, then grind using a mortar and pestle or electric coffee grinder. Set aside.

2 Heat the oil in a skillet and, when hot, add the onions and garlic. Stir-fry until they begin to brown. Stir in the shrimp paste, and continue to cook until it begins to brown. Place in a blender or food processor with the hot water and blend to a paste.

3 Put the paste into a bowl with the roasted spices, add the sweet soy sauce, lime juice, chili powder, salt, and pepper. Mix well.

Makes 1 cup

Lemongrass and ginger marinade

This Southeast Asian-inspired marinade is especially delicious on chicken or pork. Galangal, also known as Thai ginger, is similar in flavor to "regular" ginger, and can be found in Asian markets.

2 lemongrass stalks, inside soft part only, sliced finely	2 cloves garlic, chopped finely
2-inch piece gingerroot, or galangal if available, peeled and chopped	2 tbsp peanut oil
	2 tbsp fish sauce
2 to 4 Thai chiles, according to taste	2 tbsp packed brown sugar
	1 tbsp lime juice
1 red bell pepper, seeded and chopped finely	4 tbsp water
1 medium onion, chopped finely	

Place the ingredients in a blender or food processor and blend to a smooth paste.

Makes ¾ cup

Opposite Lemongrass and ginger marinade

Teriyaki red wine marinade

Teriyaki is a Japanese soy sauce that's very smooth and deep flavored, making it ideal for marinating. In Japanese, *teri* means "sunshine" and *yaki* means "roast" or "grilled," so what could be more suitable for barbecuing? This marinade is particularly good with beef, lamb, and duck.

4 tbsp Teriyaki sauce

4 tbsp red wine

1 tbsp sesame oil

1 tbsp finely chopped gingerroot

2 large cloves garlic, chopped finely

Combine the ingredients in a medium bowl and mix well.

Makes ½ cup

Cilantro, lime, and vermouth marinade

Dry white vermouth is flavored with blends of herbs and spices. As each producer has their own special blend, the taste (and quality) of vermouth varies between brands. If you would like to add a bit of "heat," add a drop or two of Tabasco sauce.

3 tbsp finely chopped cilantro

Finely shredded zest and juice of 2 limes

2 tbsp dry white vermouth

2 cloves garlic, minced

¼ cup olive oil

Tabasco sauce (optional)

Freshly ground black pepper

Combine all the ingredients in a small bowl and mix well.

Makes ¾ cup

Hot soy sauce

This glaze is precooked and then brushed over the food during the last few minutes of cooking. It goes well with fish, seafood, chicken, or pork.

2 tbsp olive oil

2 fresh red chiles, seeded, and chopped finely

2 tsp shredded gingerroot

2 cloves garlic, pressed

¼ pint dry white wine

4 tbsp soy sauce

2 tbsp packed dark brown sugar

2 tsp cornstarch

1 tbsp lemon juice

1 Heat the oil in a skillet and add the chile, ginger, and garlic. Cook, stirring frequently, 1 to 2 minutes. Do not brown.

2 In a separate bowl, whisk together the wine, soy sauce, brown sugar, and cornstarch and add to the skillet.

3 Bring to a boil, stirring, until thickened. Pour the sauce into a bowl and let cool.

4 Stir the lemon juice into the cooled sauce.

5 Brush the glaze over the food you are cooking during the final 15 minutes of grilling. Cook over medium heat to prevent the glaze from browning too quickly.

Makes ½ cup

Above left Teriyaki red wine marinade **right** Hot soy sauce

Sesame lime marinade

The sesame oil in this marinade creates a wonderfully nutty flavor that is balanced by the citric tartness of the lime juice. Use this mixture on chicken, fish, and seafood.

2 tbsp sesame oil
2 tbsp rice vinegar
2 tbsp lime juice
2 tbsp light soy sauce
2 tsp sugar

Combine the ingredients in a medium bowl and mix well.

Makes ¹/₂ cup

White wine marinade

This classic wine marinade imparts a delicate action on chicken and fish. The cilantro will give it a peppery kick. You could substitute parsley if you prefer a very subtle marinade.

4 tbsp dry white wine
2 tbsp lemon juice
6 tbsp olive oil
1 garlic clove, pressed
1 small red onion, chopped finely
2 tbsp finely chopped cilantro
2 bay leaves, crumbled
Freshly ground black pepper

Combine the ingredients in a medium bowl and mix well.

Makes 1 cup

Hoisin marinade

Some people think of hoisin sauce as "Chinese ketchup" because, like ketchup, it's a popular condiment. But that's where the similarities end – hoisin is a mixture of soy beans, garlic, chiles, and spices with no tomatoes to be found.

1 cup hoisin sauce
3 tbsp rice vinegar
2 tbsp light soy sauce
4 cloves garlic, chopped finely
¹/₄ tsp five-spice powder
2 tbsp sesame oil
Dash of Tabasco sauce

Combine the ingredients in a small bowl and mix well.

Makes 1¹/₂ cups

FISH AND SEAFOOD 3

Spice-rubbed tilapia with mango and red onion salsa

Tilapia is a farm-raised fish with a light and slightly sweet flavor. This dish goes very well with couscous and grilled asparagus.

2 lbs tilapia (filleted)

FOR THE SALSA

1 ripe mango, peeled and diced

1 red bell pepper, seeded and diced

1 red onion, diced

3 tbsp finely chopped cilantro

1 tsp minced garlic

⅓ cup fresh lime juice

¼ cup pineapple juice

1 tbsp seeded and finely chopped serrano chile

Sea salt and freshly ground black pepper to taste

¼ cup olive oil

FOR THE SPICE RUB

1 tbsp ground cumin, toasted

1 tbsp ground coriander

1 tbsp sweet Hungarian paprika

1 tbsp sea salt

1 tbsp freshly ground black pepper

1 Mix all the salsa ingredients in a medium bowl and blend well. Cover and set aside.

2 Combine all the rub ingredients in a small bowl and mix well.

3 Brush the tilapia with the olive oil. Rub the spice mixture onto the oil-coated tilapia. Place the tilapia in a fish-grilling basket and grill over medium heat, 3 to 4 minutes per side, or until the fish flakes easily with a fork. Transfer to a platter or individual plates, top with the salsa, and serve.

Serves 4

Mackerel with spicy tomato jam

Mackerel is a very oily, medium-firm fish that contains a high level of vitamin A, so this comforting dish is very good for you. Mackerel is at its best around spring and summer.

1 lb tomatoes, skinned, seeded, and chopped

1 medium Spanish onion, diced

½ cup apple jelly

¼ cup cider vinegar

1 tbsp chopped tarragon

1 tsp sea salt

½ to 1 tsp crushed red chile pepper

Four 8-oz mackerel fillets, cleaned, with heads removed but with skin left on

Olive oil

Garlic salt and freshly ground black pepper to taste

Sprigs tarragon and orange slices, to garnish

1 Combine the tomato, onion, jelly, vinegar, tarragon, salt, and chile pepper in a medium saucepan. Bring to a boil over a medium-high heat. Reduce the heat to medium-low and cook, stirring frequently, 35 to 45 minutes or until thick. Cool the jam to room temperature.

2 Season the mackerel with salt and pepper and brush the skin with olive oil. Grill, skin side down, covered, over medium-hot heat, 5 minutes on each side. Do not turn the fish or overcook it.

3 To serve, top each fillet with 2 tablespoons of tomato jam and season to taste. Garnish with tarragon and orange slices.

Serves 4

Opposite Mackerel with spicy tomato jam

Swordfish kabobs with bay leaf and lemon marinade

For those of you who like swordfish, this recipe is a real treat. If you serve it at your next party, your guests will ask for the recipe.

FOR THE MARINADE

1 tsp shredded lemon zest

1/4 cup fresh lemon juice

1/4 cup olive oil

2 cloves garlic, pressed

2 tsp packed light brown sugar

1 tsp sea salt

1 tsp freshly ground black pepper

8 bay leaves

Four 1/2-inch thick slices lemon, each cut in half

1 lb swordfish steaks, cut into 1 1/2-inch squares (approximately 20 pieces)

4 large cherry tomatoes

Half yellow bell pepper, cut into four

4 metal skewers

Olive oil

1 Combine all the marinade ingredients except the swordfish in a resealable plastic bag. Add the swordfish, seal, and turn to coat. Marinate in the refrigerator for 1 hour, turning the bag occasionally.

2 Remove the swordfish from the bag and reserve the marinade. Thread five pieces of swordfish onto each skewer, alternating with a bay leaf and lemon slice taken from the marinade, along with a cherry tomato and pepper square. Keep 1/4 cup of the marinade for basting and discard the rest.

3 Thoroughly brush the kabobs with olive oil and grill over medium-hot heat, basting occasionally. Turn onto each of the four sides, about 3 minutes per side, or until the fish flakes easily with a fork.

Serves 4

Opposite Grilled swordfish steaks

Grilled swordfish steaks

I like to serve this swordfish with a fruit salsa, and it also goes very well with blush wine.

1 tbsp ground cumin, toasted

1 tsp sea salt

1/2 tsp freshly ground black pepper

1/4 tsp chipotle chili powder

2 tbsp olive oil

Four 6 to 8 oz swordfish steaks

2 tbsp finely chopped parsley

1 lime, quartered

1 Combine the cumin, salt, pepper, and chipotle powder in a small bowl and blend well.

2 Generously sprinkle the seasoning over the steaks, gently pressing the spices into the fish. Be sure to season both sides. Loosely cover the steaks and set aside for 15 to 20 minutes.

3 Pour the oil onto a small plate. Dip each steak in the olive oil and grill over medium-high heat, 4 to 5 minutes per side or until the fish flakes easily with a fork. Transfer to a platter or individual plates and garnish with parsley and a lime wedge.

Serves 4

Jamaican jerked sea bass with tropical salsa

Spicy, spicy, spicy – that's the best way to describe this fish. You can make it as hot or as mild as you like by adjusting the quantity of hot peppers you use.

FOR THE JERK MARINADE
¼ cup white vinegar
Zest of 1 lime
Juice of 2 limes
3 tbsp vegetable oil
2 cloves garlic, chopped
½ to 2 Scotch bonnet chile peppers, seeded and chopped finely
1 tbsp sugar
2 tsp shredded gingerroot
2 tsp allspice
2 tsp ground thyme
1 tsp ground cinnamon
½ tsp sea salt
½ tsp freshly ground black pepper
½ tsp cayenne pepper

FOR THE TROPICAL SALSA
1 cup diced pineapple
¾ cup diced mango
⅔ cup diced red bell pepper
½ cup peeled, seeded, and diced plum tomatoes
⅓ cup diced red onion
⅓ cup diced cucumber
2 tbsp fresh lime juice
2 tbsp chopped fresh mint
1 tbsp chopped cilantro
1 tbsp chopped parsley
1 tbsp seeded, and chopped canned chipotle peppers in adobo sauce
Sea salt and freshly ground black pepper
Six 6 to 8 oz sea bass fillets

1 Combine the marinade ingredients in a blender until smooth. Place the sea bass in a glass dish and add the marinade, making sure the fish is well coated. Cover and marinate in the refrigerator for 30 to 45 minutes.

2 Combine the salsa ingredients in a bowl and toss gently to blend. Cover and refrigerate for at least 1 hour to allow the flavors to develop.

4 Remove the sea bass from the marinade. Grill over medium-hot heat for 4 to 5 minutes per side. Serve, topped with salsa.

Serves 6

Barbecue-glazed red snapper

Red snapper is a very tasty and popular fish. Buy your fish from a fish outlet you can trust to ensure you'll be using the freshest fish for this recipe.

1 small onion, chopped
1 tbsp packed dark brown sugar
¼ cup cider vinegar
2 tbsp ketchup
2 tbsp prepared yellow mustard
1 tbsp Worcestershire sauce
1 tsp chili powder
½ tsp sea salt
½ tsp freshly ground black pepper
¼ tsp ground cloves
¼ tsp cayenne pepper
1½ lbs red snapper fillets
Olive oil

1 Combine all the ingredients except the fish and olive oil in a small saucepan over medium-high heat. Bring to a boil. Reduce the heat and simmer, stirring occasionally, until the sauce is reduced to a syrup-like consistency, about 3 to 4 minutes. Strain and chill the syrup.

2 Place the red snapper in a glass baking dish and thoroughly coat with the syrup by brushing or spooning it over the fillets. Cover and marinate in the refrigerator for 1 hour.

3 Brush both sides of the red snapper lightly with olive oil and grill over medium-hot heat, basting with the remaining syrup, 4 to 5 minutes per side or until the fish flakes easily with a fork.

Serves 4 to 6

Seared tuna with Cuban Mojito sauce

This simple grilled tuna dish is twice-flavored, first with a spicy marinade, then with homemade Cuban Mojito sauce, an orange-lime-garlic blend that can be used as a marinade for fish or as a sauce after cooking. Grilling is the perfect way to cook tuna, because the outside is seared, leaving the inside pink and juicy.

4 tuna steaks (6 oz each)

3 cloves garlic

1 tsp sea salt

1/2 tsp cumin

Juice of 1 orange

Juice of 1 lime

Freshly ground black pepper

Cayenne pepper to taste

2 tbsp olive oil, or as needed

FOR THE MOJITO SAUCE

1 cup orange juice

Juice of 1 lime

1/2 cup olive oil

3 cloves garlic, minced

2 tbsp finely chopped bacon

1 tbsp dry sherry

1 tsp salt

1 tsp dried oregano

1 tsp ground cumin

1 tbsp grated gingerroot

1 Combine the garlic, salt, cumin, orange and lime juice, black pepper, and cayenne pepper in a medium bowl and mix well.

2 Place the tuna in a glass baking dish. Pour the marinade over the tuna, turning to coat all sides. Cover and let marinate about 30 minutes.

3 Remove the tuna from the marinade and pat dry.

4 Meanwhile, prepare the mojito sauce. Place all the mojito sauce ingredients in a jar and shake well until thoroughly blended.

5 Grill the tuna over high heat, about 1 to 2 minutes per side. Serve with the mojito sauce.

Serves 4

Spice-crusted tuna with vegetables and tofu

Cooking time for the tuna will depend on how thick the steaks are and how rare you like your fish. Allow between 1 to 2 minutes per side over a fairly brisk heat.

4 tuna steaks

2 tbsp coriander seeds, finely crushed

1 tsp chili sauce

2 tsp gingerroot purée

1 1/4 cups trimmed green beans

1 bunch asparagus

1 bunch scallions, trimmed

3 tbsp vegetable or peanut oil

2 tbsp unsalted butter

9 oz firm tofu, cut into 2-inch long sticks

Juice of 2 limes

Small bunch of cilantro

4 tbsp chopped parsley

1 Place the tuna steaks in a glass baking dish. Combine the coriander seeds, chili sauce, and ginger purée in a small bowl and spread over the fish. Cover and marinate in the refrigerator for about 1 hour.

2 Steam the green beans, asparagus, and scallions for 5 minutes until just tender. Keep them warm in a low oven.

3 Melt the oil and butter in a saucepan over low heat. Transfer to a shallow dish, and dip the spice-side of the tuna steaks into the mixture. Grill over hot heat, spice-side down, 2 to 3 minutes, turn, and then cook an additional 1 to 2 minutes. Or, cook to the doneness you desire.

4 Toss the tofu with the remaining butter and oil and grill over medium-high heat until heated through, 2 to 3 minutes. Remove from the heat and squeeze the lime juice over the tofu. To serve, arrange the vegetables and tofu on serving plates with the tuna steaks on top. Tuck a few cilantro leaves among the vegetables and tofu, and scatter with parsley.

Serves 4

Chile cod and avocado salsa

This is a dish with a real Mexican theme, and it is fairly hot and spicy.

4 skinless cod fillets

FOR THE AVOCADO SALSA
1 large, ripe avocado
2 tbsp fresh lemon juice
1 tomato, peeled, seeded, and chopped
1 onion, chopped finely
Freshly ground black pepper to taste

FOR THE MARINADE
1 tbsp lime juice
1 onion, chopped
1 red bell pepper, chopped
2 cloves garlic, minced
2 red chiles, chopped
2 tbsp light soy sauce
²/₃ cup fish stock
1 tsp chili powder

1 To make the avocado salsa, halve and pit the avocado. Peel and place in a blender or food processor with the lemon juice and blend until smooth, about 10 seconds. Transfer to a bowl and add the tomato, onion, and pepper. Cover and chill in the refrigerator until needed.

2 Place the cod fillets on four squares of heavy duty foil. Put the remaining marinade ingredients in a blender and blend for 10 seconds. Spread the marinade onto the cod and close the parcels around the fish, being sure to secure the seams.

3 Grill over medium heat 10 to 15 minutes. Serve with the avocado salsa.

Serves 4

Salmon and tomato packets

Wrap salmon fillets in foil and cook them on the grill, and you'll be well on your way to a dinner with almost nothing to clean. Just crumple up the foil, throw it away, and the dishes are done.

2 tbsp unsalted butter
Six 1¹/₂-inch thick skinless salmon fillets
6 tomatoes, cut into wedges
6 scallions (white and green parts) chopped
2 tbsp olive oil

1 tbsp fresh lemon juice
1 tsp superfine sugar
Whole or chopped herbs, such as dill, cilantro, and parsley

1 Cut six large squares of heavy duty foil. Butter the foil and lay a salmon fillet on each square. Top with some tomato wedges and a sprinkling of scallions.

2 Whisk together the oil, lemon juice, and sugar. Drizzle it over the salmon. Add a few sprigs of herbs to the parcels.

3 Close the parcels, being sure to secure the seams. Grill over medium-hot heat, turning occasionally, 8 to 10 minutes. Carefully open the parcels to avoid the steam, and serve immediately.

Serves 6

Opposite Salmon and tomato packets

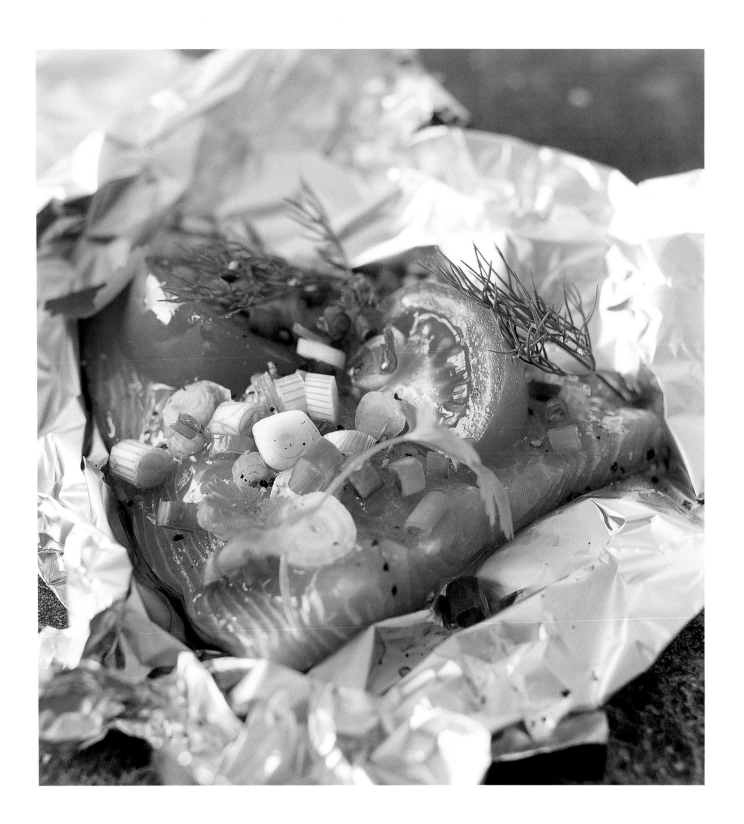

Orange-and-chile marinated sardines

Sardines cooked this way are simply delicious. Use lime juice instead of orange, if you prefer. Use a grill basket designed for fish if you have one.

8 to 12 fresh sardines, cleaned

½ cup fresh orange juice

4 tbsp olive oil

1 to 4 jalapeño chiles, seeded and sliced finely

1 tbsp packed light brown sugar

Sprigs of fresh rosemary

Orange wedges

1 Wipe or lightly rinse the sardines and pat dry with paper towels. Place in a glass baking dish.

2 Combine the orange juice, oil, chile, and brown sugar in a small bowl. Pour the mixture over the sardines and add some springs of rosemary. Cover and marinate in the refrigerator at least 2 hours, turning occasionally.

3 Grill the sardines over medium heat, basting with the marinade at least once during cooking, 3 to 4 minutes or until cooked through.

4 Garnish with orange wedges and sprigs of rosemary.

Serves 4

Right Orange-and-chile marinated sardines

Stuffed red mullet

Grape leaves are usually preserved in brine, so it's important to soak them thoroughly before use.

12 to 16 grape leaves, depending upon size

Boiling water

4 small red mullet or other small whole fish, cleaned and scaled

2 tbsp olive oil

4 scallions (green and white parts), chopped

½ cup dried apricots, chopped finely

2 tbsp chopped hazelnuts

1 tbsp shredded orange zest

1 tbsp chopped fresh dill

½ cup fresh bread crumbs

Sea salt and freshly ground black pepper to taste

1 medium egg yolk

2 to 3 tbsp orange juice

Olive oil

1 Cover the grape leaves with boiling water and let sit for 20 minutes. Drain and rinse thoroughly with boiling water. Pat dry with paper towels and set aside.

2 Heat 2 teaspoons of the oil in a skillet and sauté the scallions for 2 minutes. Remove from the heat and add the apricots, hazelnuts, orange zest, dill, bread crumbs, salt, and pepper. Mix in the egg yolk and enough orange juice to give the mixture a stiff consistency.

3 Use the stuffing to fill the cavities of the fish. Wrap each fish in the grape leaves, encasing them completely, and secure with either soaked twine or toothpicks.

4 Oil the grill with olive oil and cook the fish over a medium heat, 4 to 6 minutes per side, or until done and the grape leaves are charred.

5 Remove the twine or toothpicks and serve.

Serves 4

Grilled halibut steak with Caribbean marinade

Halibut steaks are a great alternative to salmon steaks, especially if you want a less oily fish. They are thick enough to stand up to grilling without the aid of a grill basket, which can't be said for a lot of other white-fleshed fish.

2 tbsp red wine vinegar

1 large onion, grated

2 tbsp tomato paste

4 cloves garlic, minced

2 tsp packed brown sugar

1 to 2 tbsp red chili paste (optional)

2 tsp anchovy paste

4 halibut steaks (9 oz each)

1 Combine all the ingredients except the halibut in a small bowl and mix well.

2 Place the fish in a glass baking dish. Pour the marinade over the fish, turning to coat all sides. Cover and marinate for 1 hour.

3 Remove the halibut from the dish, reserving some of the marinade. Grill over hot heat for about 6 minutes per side, brushing with the marinade while cooking.

Serves 4

Barbecued halibut steaks

Serve this fish with a fruit salsa, a tartar sauce made with mayonnaise, and hard-cooked eggs, or even hollandaise sauce. It's very versatile and very delicious.

2 tbsp unsalted butter

2 tbsp packed light brown sugar

3 cloves garlic, pressed

2 tbsp fresh lemon juice

2 tbsp soy sauce

1/2 tsp freshly ground black pepper

1/4 tsp cayenne pepper

1 1/2 lbs halibut steak

1 Combine all the ingredients except the fish in a small saucepan and heat until the butter melts and the sugar dissolves. Cool to room temperature.

2 Coat the halibut with the sauce and grill over medium-hot heat, frequently basting with the sauce, 5 to 7 minutes per side, or until the fish flakes easily with a fork.

Serves 4

Grilled trout with bacon

An unusual combination; however, the salt of the bacon gives the trout a lip-smacking edge.

4 trout, at least 12 oz each

Sea salt and freshly ground black pepper to taste

8 bacon slices

4 bay leaves

1 Season the trout with the salt and pepper. Wrap two slices of bacon around each trout and tuck a bay leaf inside a fold in the bacon, but be sure the bay leaf is also touching the fish.

2 Brush the rack with oil and grill the trout over hot heat, 4 to 6 minutes per side. Serve immediately.

Serves 4

Opposite Grilled halibut steak with Caribbean marinade

Crab cakes with honey mustard sauce

As an accompaniment to these special crab cakes, I suggest serving foil-wrapped squash and apples with brown sugar (see page 124), along side a tossed salad or coleslaw.

FOR THE HONEY MUSTARD SAUCE

¼ cup light honey

¼ cup Dijon mustard

1 shallot, minced

2 tsp sugar

¼ tsp curry powder

¾ tsp celery seed

2 tbsp rice vinegar

2 to 3 drops Tabasco sauce

FOR THE CRAB CAKES

1 lb fresh or canned crabmeat, picked clean of shell

⅓ cup mayonnaise

2 tsp dried mustard

1 tsp Worcestershire sauce

¼ tsp seasoned salt

¼ tsp white pepper

¼ cup diced pimento

¼ cup diced green bell pepper

¼ cup finely chopped onion

⅓ to ½ cup fresh, unseasoned bread crumbs

Olive oil

1 Combine all the honey mustard sauce ingredients in a small bowl and blend well. Set aside.

2 Flake the crabmeat with a fork. In a large bowl, whisk together the mayonnaise, mustard, Worcestershire sauce, salt, and pepper. Add the crabmeat, pimento, bell pepper, and onion. Fold in the bread crumbs and blend well. Add more bread crumbs if needed to hold the mixture together. Form into 6 to 8 cakes.

3 Place the crab cakes on a cookie sheet and refrigerate for 2 to 3 hours or until firm. Brush both sides of the cakes with olive oil and grill over medium-hot heat, 4 to 5 minutes per side or until done. Use a grill basket if you have one, as it makes turning much easier. Serve with the honey mustard sauce.

Serves 4

Crab quesadillas with mango salsa

This dish is excellent as a starter before dinner, or served as an appetizer for your next get-together with friends.

FOR THE MANGO SALSA

1 ripe mango, peeled and diced

2 plum tomatoes, seeded and diced

3 scallions, thinly sliced (green and white parts)

Juice of 1 lime

2 tbsp chopped fresh mint

2 tbsp raspberry vinegar

½ tsp sea salt

¼ tsp freshly ground black pepper

FOR THE QUESADILLAS

1½ cups shredded cooked crabmeat

6 oz Monterey Jack or Cheddar cheese, shredded

1 avocado, diced

½ cup chopped scallions (white and green parts)

⅓ cup chopped cilantro

¼ cup chopped, roasted red bell pepper

2 tbsp fresh lime juice

Sea salt and freshly ground black pepper

2 tbsp olive oil

Six 8-inch flour tortillas

1 Combine all the salsa ingredients in a medium bowl and gently toss. Cover and chill at least 1 hour so the flavors can develop.

2 For the quesadillas, combine all the ingredients except the oil and tortillas in a medium bowl and gently toss, being sure to mix the ingredients thoroughly.

3 Brush one side of two tortillas with olive oil. Place one tortilla, oil side down, on a grill that is medium hot. Spread with the crabmeat mixture and then top with the second tortilla, oil side up, pressing down on the tortilla with a spatula. Place on the grill, cover, and cook about 4 to 5 minutes. Turn the quesadilla, and cook, covered, for another 3 to 4 minutes or until the cheese has melted. Transfer to a board and cut in half, then cut each half into pie-shaped pieces. Serve with the mango salsa.

Serves 4

Above left Crab cakes with honey mustard sauce **right** Crab quesadillas with mango salsa

Grilled oysters Palatine

These oysters are one of my party favorites – they're so easy to make. You and your guests can stand around the grill while they cook. Just make sure you have a good lager in your hands.

FOR THE FILLING

2 tbsp unsalted butter

1 lb chopped frozen spinach, thawed

1 tsp sea salt

½ tsp white pepper

¼ tsp ground mace

FOR THE SAUCE

1½ sticks unsalted butter

5 large egg yolks

2 tbsp fresh lemon juice

2 tbsp dry vermouth

2 dashes Tabasco Sauce, or to taste

Sea salt to taste

1 tsp curry powder, or to taste

24 oysters on the half shell, drained of most of their liquor

1 For the filling, place the butter and spinach in a pan over medium heat and cook, stirring occasionally, until the spinach is tender, about 15 minutes. Strain in a colander, and squeeze out excess liquid with the back of a spoon. Season with pepper, mace, and salt and set aside to cool completely.

2 For the sauce, melt the butter in a small pan over medium heat until foamy. Do not let it brown. Put the egg yolks, lemon juice, vermouth, Tabasco sauce, and salt in a blender. Blend for 5 seconds at medium speed. Increase to high speed and slowly pour in half the melted butter while the blender is running, for about 30 seconds. Sprinkle the curry powder over the emulsion. Blend again at high and slowly add the remaining butter while the blender is running, about 15 seconds. Taste the sauce and adjust the curry powder if necessary.

3 Divide the spinach mixture among the 24 shells, place an oyster on top, and add a dollop of hollandaise sauce. Grill the oysters over hot heat for about 5 minutes or until they are bubbly and cooked.

Serves 4 to 6

Grilled Cheddar oysters

As long as there are oysters around, I'll be there to grill them. These are delicious and slightly unusual. They make a great treat accompanied by a crisp white wine.

FOR THE FILLING

1 tsp arrowroot

1 tbsp cold water

2 tbsp butter

1 leek, cleaned and sliced

2 cloves garlic, pressed

1 ear fresh corn, husked, grilled, and kernels cut off the cob

1 cup heavy cream

Pinch of mace

½ cup shredded sharp Cheddar cheese

1 leek, sliced finely, to garnish

Sea salt and freshly ground black pepper to taste

FOR THE TOPPING

2 slices smoked bacon, cooked crisp and crumbled

1 cup plain bread crumbs

2 tbsp olive oil

24 oysters on the half shell

1 Mix the arrowroot and cold water and set aside.

2 Melt the butter in a saucepan and sauté the leek, garlic, and corn over a medium heat until the leek is soft and tender. Add the cream and mace and bring to a boil. Reduce the heat and simmer. Thicken slightly by adding the arrowroot and water mixture, stirring the mixture again before adding it to the pan. Remove from the heat and blend in the cheese with a wire whisk. Season with salt and pepper.

3 Combine the topping ingredients except for the oysters in a medium bowl and blend well.

4 To assemble, top each oyster in its shell with some of the filling and sprinkle with some of the topping. Grill over a medium heat for 5 minutes, covered, until the oysters are hot and bubbly. Serve garnished with shredded leek and crushed sea salt, if desired.

Serves 4 to 6

Opposite Grilled oysters Palatine

Asian grilled shrimp with honey-tea dipping sauce

I like serving this Asian delight on a bed of citrus rice fried in a little ginger and garlic. To make extra-strong tea, simply use two tea bags with the usual amount of boiling water for one cup.

1 cup extra-strong orange spiced tea, cooled

½ cup honey

½ cup sweet rice vinegar

1 tbsp fresh lemon juice

1 tbsp shredded gingerroot

1 clove garlic, pressed

1 tsp ground coriander

½ tsp ground black pepper

1½ lbs medium shrimp, peeled and deveined, with tails left on

Garlic salt to taste

4 scallions, thinly sliced (white and green parts)

Orange wedges

8 metal skewers

1 Combine the tea, honey, vinegar, lemon juice, ginger, garlic, coriander, and pepper and blend well. Reserve ½ cup of the marinade, cover, and set aside.

2 Place the shrimp and the marinade in a resealable plastic bag, seal, and turn to coat. Marinate in the refrigerator for at least 30 to 45 minutes.

3 Remove the shrimp from the bag, discarding the marinade. Thread the shrimp onto 8 skewers, dividing them evenly, and alternating with orange wedges. Grill over medium heat, turning only once, for 4 to 6 minutes or until the shrimp are just pink and firm to the touch. Be careful not to overcook. Season the cooked shrimp with garlic salt to taste.

4 To prepare the dipping sauce, add the reserved marinade to a pan. Bring to a boil over medium heat and reduce the sauce slightly, about 3 to 5 minutes. Stir in the scallion. Serve hot.

Serves 4 to 6

Opposite Asian grilled shrimp with honey-tea dipping sauce

Creamy lobster sauce with fettuccine

To prepare lobster for this delectable pasta dish, it is first removed from the shell, then grilled, and coated in garlic butter. Your mouth will water as you read the recipe.

½ cup white wine

2 tbsp sherry wine vinegar

½ cup fish stock

¼ cup finely chopped shallots

2 cups heavy cream

2 ripe avocados, diced

8 plum tomatoes, peeled and diced

1 stick unsalted butter, softened

2 cloves garlic, pressed

1 lb fettuccine pasta

Sea salt and freshly ground black pepper to taste

One 1 to 1¼ lb lobster tail

Chopped fresh parsley, to garnish

1 Combine the wine, vinegar, fish stock, and shallots in a medium pan over medium heat. Bring to a boil stirring continually until the liquid has reduced its volume to ½ cup. Add the cream, avocado, and tomatoes and bring back to a boil. Reduce the heat and simmer until reduced and thickened, about 2 to 3 minutes. Season with salt and pepper.

2 Combine the butter and garlic in a small pan and melt over medium-low heat. Set aside.

3 Cook the pasta in a large pot of boiling, salted water until tender but still firm (al dente). Drain, set aside, and keep warm.

4 Split the lobster tail, devein it, and remove the meat from the shell. Thoroughly brush the lobster meat on all sides with the garlic butter. Grill over medium-hot heat, 4 to 5 minutes per side, or until the meat is opaque and white. Remove from the grill, chop the meat, and add it to the cream sauce. Blend well.

5 Transfer the warm pasta to a serving platter and top with the lobster sauce. Garnish with the parsley and serve.

Serves 4 to 6

Above left Scallops with zucchini and tomato pasta **right** Scallop and shrimp brochettes

Scallops with zucchini and tomato pasta

Grilled scallops are sweet, tasty, and easy to cook. Here is a great meal that can be made in about 30 minutes or less.

1 lb linguini pasta
¼ cup olive oil
4 cloves garlic, minced
2 medium zucchini, diced
1 tsp sea salt
1 tsp freshly ground black pepper

½ tsp crushed red pepper
1 cup chopped basil leaves
4 plum tomatoes, diced
1½ lbs sea scallops
Olive oil
2 tbsp freshly shredded Parmesan

1 Cook the pasta in a large pot of boiling, salted water until tender but still firm (*al dente*).

2 In a skillet on the stovetop or on your grill, heat the oil and sauté the garlic for 1 minute. Add the zucchini, salt, pepper, and red pepper and sauté over a medium heat for 8 to 10 minutes or until tender and crisp. Add the basil and tomato and simmer for 5 to 7 minutes. Remove from the heat and keep warm.

3 Brush the scallops with olive oil and grill over medium-hot heat, 3 minutes per side, until the scallops are opaque. Remove the scallops, quarter them, and add to the sauce mixture.

4 Transfer the pasta to a large serving platter or bowl. Pour the sauce over the cooked pasta and sprinkle with the Parmesan.

Serves 4 to 6

Scallop and shrimp brochettes

Scallops and shrimp are a no-fail shellfish combination. This herb-infused marinade adds just enough flavor to these tasty beauties. Keep a careful eye on the brochettes because the scallops and shrimp don't take long to cook.

FOR THE MARINADE
1 cup dry white wine
2 tbsp balsamic vinegar
2 tbsp fresh lemon juice
¼ cup vegetable oil
1 tbsp finely chopped tarragon
1 tsp finely chopped basil
1 tsp finely chopped thyme
1 tsp finely chopped oregano
1 tsp sugar
Sea salt and freshly ground black pepper

1 to 2 lbs scallops, shucked and rinsed
1 to 2 lbs shrimp, peeled and deveined
2 sticks unsalted butter, melted
2 tbsp fresh lemon juice
2 tsp freshly ground black pepper
1 tsp paprika
1 lemon, cut into wedges
6 metal skewers

1 Combine the wine, vinegar, lemon juice, oil, herbs, sugar, salt, and pepper in a glass bowl and mix well with a wire whisk. Place the scallops and shrimp in the marinade, tossing to coat evenly. Cover and marinate in the refrigerator for 30 minutes to 1 hour.

2 Drain the scallops and shrimp and thread them onto long metal skewers, threading the scallops through their diameter. Combine the melted butter and lemon juice. Brush the scallops and shrimp with the butter mixture and season with pepper and paprika.

3 Grill over hot heat, basting with the butter-lemon mixture every 3 to 4 minutes, 6 to 8 minutes per side, or until done, being careful not to overcook.

Serves 6 to 8

Grilled octopus and peppers

The first time I had the pleasure of eating octopus, I was in Hawaii. It took a little work to make, but the results were worth the effort. Once you try this dish, I think you'll agree.

1 small octopus (about 1 lb)

½ cup fresh lemon juice

¼ cup olive oil

4 cloves garlic, pressed

½ tsp dried oregano

½ tsp dried marjoram

1 tsp sea salt

½ tsp freshly ground black pepper

2 tbsp olive oil

1 green bell pepper

1 red bell pepper

1 yellow bell pepper

FOR THE DRESSING

½ cup olive oil

2 tbsp balsamic vinegar

1 tbsp fresh lemon juice

1 tbsp sugar

2 cloves garlic, pressed

1 tbsp finely chopped parsley

½ tsp sea salt

½ tsp freshly ground black pepper

Lemon wedges, to serve

1 Cut the octopus into strips or leave whole if small. Rinse well and place in a glass bowl. Add the lemon juice, oil, garlic, oregano, marjoram, salt, and pepper. Cover and marinate in the refrigerator for 24 hours, stirring occasionally.

2 Brush the skin of the peppers with 2 tablespoons of olive oil. Grill over hot heat until the skin blisters all over, approximately 4 to 5 minutes. Remove from the heat and place in a sealed paper bag. Let rest about 20 minutes.

3 For the dressing, combine all the ingredients in a small bowl and blend well.

4 Remove the peppers from the bag and, using a towel, rub off the skins. Seed and remove the membranes. Slice the peppers into strips and arrange on a serving plate, alternating the colors. Drizzle with half the dressing and set aside.

5 Remove the octopus from the bowl and reserve the marinade. Grill the octopus over hot heat, turning frequently and basting with the reserved marinade, 15 to 20 minutes. Remove from the grill, cut into bite-sized pieces, and pile in the middle of the plate of peppers. Drizzle with the remaining dressing and serve, accompanied with lemon wedges to squeeze over.

Serves 2 to 4

Paella

A one-dish meal, paella provides a wonderful variety of tastes and textures. Let people help themselves straight from the pan. If you have a small grill, cook the rice in advance, add the oil and lemon dressing, and let it cool to room temperature. Then, cook all the extras on the grill and pile them high, hot, onto the cooled rice.

6 tbsp olive oil, plus extra for brushing

3 tbsp fresh lemon juice

2 tbsp honey

8 chicken thighs

16 large shrimp

12 oz mussels

¾ cup dry white wine, plus 3 tbsp for the mussels

½ stick unsalted butter

1 onion, chopped finely

2 red bell peppers, seeds removed and sliced

2 cloves garlic, minced

1 lb risotto rice, such as Arborio

About 4½ cups hot vegetable or chicken stock

4 tomatoes, peeled and chopped

½ tsp ground saffron

Sea salt and freshly ground pepper to taste

3 tbsp chopped parsley

Lemon wedges

1 Whisk together 3 tablespoons of the oil with the lemon juice and honey, and set aside. Brush the chicken thighs and the shrimp with this dressing. Pile the mussels onto a large piece of heavy duty foil and add 3 tablespoons of the wine and the butter. Wrap loosely (you may need to allow space for the mussels to expand as they open), close the parcel and gather the seams toward the top.

2 Heat the remaining oil in a large paella dish or large shallow skillet and add the onion, pepper, and garlic. Cook gently, stirring frequently, until the vegetables are soft but not brown, about 10 minutes.

3 Add the rice and cook 1 to 2 minutes, stirring.

4 Pour in about one quarter of the hot stock and the ¾ cup wine. Add the tomato, saffron, salt, and pepper. Heat, stirring occasionally, until the mixture comes to a boil. Then simmer gently, adding extra hot stock each time the rice has absorbed most of the liquid, until the rice is plump and tender. Do not allow the rice to dry out completely - it should stay quite moist.

5 Meanwhile, grill the chicken thighs over medium-hot heat, turning occasionally, for 15 to 20 minutes.

6 Ten minutes after placing the chicken thighs on the grill, start to grill the parcel of mussels, seam side up, along with the shrimp. Cook, turning the shrimp occasionally (but not the foil parcel), until you can hear the mussels sizzling and the parcel feels full, and the shrimp are pink and cooked, about 10 minutes.

7 Add the oil and lemon dressing to the rice. Tear open the foil parcel and pour the mussels and their butter juices into the rice, discarding any mussels that have not opened. Add the chicken, shrimp, and parsley and stir gently. Serve immediately with lemon wedges.

Serves 8

POULTRY AND GAME 4

Blueberry grilled chicken

Blueberries are not usually associated with grilled chicken, or grilled anything for that matter, but don't let that fool you. When you taste this chicken, you'll wonder why you haven't tried this combination sooner.

**Four 4 to 5 oz boneless,
   skinless chicken breasts**

½ cup apricot jam

½ cup raspberry vinegar

¼ cup spicy brown mustard

1 tsp sea salt

**½ tsp freshly ground
   black pepper**

¼ tsp cayenne pepper

¼ cup blueberries

1 Place the jam, vinegar, mustard, salt, and black pepper in a bowl and mix until well blended. Reserve ²/₃ cup and set aside.

2 Using a sharp knife, slash criss-cross slices into the chicken flesh. Place the chicken in a glass baking dish. Pour the remaining marinade over the chicken, turning to make sure both sides are coated. Cover and let marinate in the refrigerator for 3 to 4 hours. Reserve the remaining marinade.

3 Grill the chicken over medium-hot heat, basting with the reserved marinade, 5 to 7 minutes per side or until the chicken is no longer pink in the middle.

4 Combine the blueberries with the ²/₃ cup reserved marinade in a saucepan, bring to a boil, and serve over the grilled chicken.

Serves 4

Spicy grilled chicken

This is a simple yet delicious way to make chicken. If you're new to grilling, this recipe is a good place to start because chicken legs are very forgiving and easy to cook.

½ cup vegetable oil

2 tbsp fresh lime juice

2 tbsp fresh lemon juice

2 tbsp balsamic vinegar

2 cloves garlic, pressed

1 tbsp lemon pepper

1 tsp sea salt

1 tsp lime zest

**4 chicken quarters
   (leg and thigh)**

1 Combine all the ingredients except the chicken in a small bowl and blend well. Put the chicken and the marinade in a resealable plastic bag, seal, and turn to coat. Marinate in the refrigerator for 4 hours.

2 Grill the chicken over medium heat, covered, turning as needed, for 35 to 45 minutes or until the juices run clear.

Serves 4

Opposite Blueberry grilled chicken

Above left Tex-Mex wings **right** Caribbean chicken with warm fruit salsa

Tex-Mex wings

This is an economical dish to prepare for a party, as chicken wings are inexpensive. So be ready to make double, or even more quantities, and have plenty of napkins on hand. Enjoy! To make it easier to turn the wings while grilling, try threading them onto long, flat metal skewers. Alternatively, you can also use a grill basket.

Finely shredded zest and juice of 2 oranges
1 tbsp malt vinegar
3 tbsp dark molasses
1 tbsp ground coriander

1 tbsp Tabasco, or to taste
24 chicken wings, bony tips removed
4 to 6 wooden skewers, soaked

1 Put the orange juice and zest into a large nonreactive bowl. Whisk in the vinegar, molasses, coriander, and Tabasco sauce. Add the chicken wings and toss until well coated.

2 Cover and marinate in the refrigerator for about 2 hours, stirring occasionally.

3 Remove the wings from the marinade, thread onto the wooden skewers, and grill over medium-high heat, turning occasionally and basting with the remaining marinade, 20 to 25 minutes or until crisp and cooked through.

Serves 6

Caribbean chicken with warm fruit salsa

Salsas are very popular and can be made using many different ingredients. The chile here gives a pleasant, fiery tang. Use as much of the chile as your palate can take.

FOR THE MARINADE
4 skinless chicken breasts
2 cloves garlic, pressed
½ to 1 habanero chile, seeded and finely chopped
1 tbsp shredded lime zest
2 tbsp shredded gingerroot
3 tbsp fresh lime juice
½ cup mango or orange juice
2 tbsp chopped cilantro
1 tbsp olive oil
Chopped fresh cilantro and lime wedges

FOR THE SALSA
1 firm but ripe papaya, peeled and seeded
1 small fresh pineapple peeled and sliced, or 2 to 3 slices fresh pineapple
2 firm tomatoes, seeded and chopped
4 scallions (white and green parts), trimmed and finely chopped
2 tbsp chopped cilantro

1 Make three slashes diagonally across each chicken breast and place in a glass baking dish.

2 For the marinade, combine the garlic, chile, lime zest, and ginger in a small bowl. Stir in the fruit juices and cilantro. Pour over the chicken, and coat all sides. Cover and marinate in the refrigerator for 30 minutes, stirring occasionally.

3 For the salsa, slice the papaya thickly. Brush the fruit and rack with olive oil. Grill over a medium heat until seared on each side. Remove, chop finely, and mix with the remaining salsa ingredients.

4 Drain the chicken from the marinade. Grill over medium heat, 5 to 6 minutes per side. Serve garnished with cilantro and lime wedges atop 1 to 2 spoonfuls of warm salsa.

Serves 4

Citrus-glazed chicken with pear-gorgonzola salsa

The citrus zing in this glaze brings out the sweetness of the salsa, making for a delightful contrast of flavors in every bite.

FOR THE CITRUS GLAZE

1 tbsp unsalted butter

½ cup diced red onion

¼ cup orange juice concentrate

½ cup chicken stock

2 tbsp dark rum

2 tbsp honey

2 tbsp fresh lemon juice

1 tbsp fresh thyme, crushed

1 tsp lemon zest

1 tsp sea salt

Four 4 to 5 oz skinless chicken breasts

FOR THE SALSA

3 medium firm-ripe pears, cored and diced

2 cups watercress leaves

⅓ cup thinly sliced scallions (white and green parts)

⅓ cup crumbled gorgonzola cheese

2 tbsp olive oil

2 tbsp white wine vinegar

1 Melt the butter in a skillet over medium-high heat. Add the onion and sauté until it just begins to soften, 2 to 3 minutes. Add the remaining ingredients except the chicken. Bring to a boil. Reduce the heat and simmer until the mixture is reduced by half. Strain the mixture and set aside.

2 Combine all the salsa ingredients in a medium bowl and gently toss to blend. Cover and set aside, at room temperature.

3 Brush the chicken breasts with the sauce and grill over medium-high heat, brushing frequently and turning once, until golden brown and cooked through, 4 to 5 minutes per side. Transfer to a serving platter and keep warm.

4 Place the remaining sauce in a small pan. Bring to a boil and reduce again to make a glaze, about 2 to 3 minutes. Spoon over the chicken and serve with the salsa.

Serves 4

Opposite Citrus-glazed chicken with pear-gorgonzola sauce

Grilled hot wings

These wings, although great as party food, can be a bit messy. Be sure to have plenty of napkins available for your guests. Try serving them with ranch or blue cheese dressing on the side. Yum!

FOR THE RUB

1 tbsp paprika

1 tsp seasoned salt

1 tsp garlic salt

1 tsp cayenne pepper

½ tsp lemon pepper

½ tsp white pepper

½ tsp ground cumin

24 large chicken wings, tips removed

FOR THE WING SAUCE

1 cup hot red pepper sauce

1 stick unsalted butter

2 tbsp fresh lemon juice

1 tbsp Worcestershire sauce

1 tsp garlic salt

1 tsp cayenne pepper

1 Combine all the rub ingredients in a small bowl and blend well.

2 Spread the wings out on a cookie sheet and thoroughly dust them all over with the rub.

3 Grill over medium heat, covered, turning as needed about every 7 minutes, for about 15 to 20 minutes. As they are done, remove from the grill and place in a large bowl.

4 Meanwhile, combine the wing sauce ingredients in a saucepan and heat until the butter has melted, but do not let it burn. Set aside and keep warm. Pour the sauce over the cooked wings and toss well to coat. Serve hot.

Serves 4 to 6

Chicken drumsticks with yogurt marinade

Although you might be tempted to omit one or two of the spices, don't do it. The flavor combination is essential for the success of the dish.

Generous ½ cup plain yogurt	1 tsp ground cumin
3 cloves garlic, minced	1 tsp garam masala
1-inch piece gingerroot, peeled and shredded	½ tsp chili powder
	Sea salt to taste
Juice of 1 lemon	8 chicken drumsticks
1 tsp ground turmeric	
1 tsp ground coriander	

1 Place the chicken drumsticks in a glass baking dish.

2 Combine all the marinade ingredients in a bowl and mix well. Reserve some of the marinade, and add the remainder to the chicken, turning to be sure all the pieces are coated. Cover and marinate in the refrigerator overnight, turning occasionally.

3 Grill the chicken drumsticks over medium-hot heat, turning and basting frequently with the reserved marinade, 20 minutes or until the juices run clear when the thickest part of the leg is pierced.

Serves 2 to 4

Chicken and tarragon burgers

These burgers make a sophisticated alternative to beef burgers and are ideal for an informal lunch or dinner party. Serve them with assorted relishes and French fries.

1¼ lbs fresh ground chicken	8 slices prosciutto
6 scallions, trimmed and chopped finely	Olive oil
	4 pita breads, burger buns or ciabatta rolls
¼ cup toasted pine nuts	
2 tbsp chopped tarragon	Arugula leaves
1 tbsp paprika	1 red onion, peeled and sliced thinly
1 tbsp shredded lemon zest	
Sea salt and freshly ground black pepper to taste	

1 Place the chicken, scallions, pine nuts, tarragon, paprika, lemon zest, and pepper into a food processor and process for 1 minute or until the mixture forms a ball. Remove from the processor bowl and, with dampened hands, shape into four burgers. Lightly cover the burgers and chill in the refrigerator for 30 minutes.

2 Remove from the refrigerator and wrap each burger with 2 slices of prosciutto.

3 Lightly brush the burgers with olive oil and grill over medium heat, 5 to 6 minutes per side or until done.

4 Meanwhile, split the breads, buns or rolls in half and grill, cut-side down, 1 to 2 minutes or until heated.

5 To serve, place inside the warmed bread along with some arugula and sliced onion.

Serves 4

Opposite Chicken and tarragon burgers

Grilled chicken with raspberry-balsamic glaze

Chicken halves are whole chickens that have been cut into two pieces of approximately equal weight. They're great when you want the flavor of a whole chicken, but might not have the time to cook a whole bird.

FOR THE RUB

3 tbsp onion salt

1 tsp freshly ground black pepper

1 tsp dried basil

½ tsp dried thyme

¼ tsp ground celery seed

2 half chickens (3½ to 4 lbs)

FOR THE GLAZE

1 cup seedless raspberry preserve

¼ cup balsamic vinegar

1 tbsp orange-flavored liqueur, such as Triple Sec or Curaçao

1 tsp sea salt

½ tsp freshly ground black pepper

1 Combine the rub ingredients in a small bowl and blend well. Set aside.

2 Rinse the chicken and pat dry with paper towels. Thoroughly season the chicken with the rub and set aside.

3 Combine the glaze ingredients in a saucepan and cook over medium heat, stirring with a wire whisk until blended, about 10 minutes.

4 Grill the chicken over medium heat, skin side down, covered, turning every 10 to 15 minutes, for about 1 hour. Brush with the glaze and cook for 5 to 7 minutes more, repeating the glazing at least one more time, or as desired.

Serves 2 to 4

Sweet-and-sour chicken wings

The chicken wings are threaded onto kabob sticks for easy turning on the barbecue. Alternatively, cook them in a grill basket. Serve with grilled yellow bell peppers.

1 medium onion, chopped

2 cloves garlic

1 small green bell pepper, seeded and chopped

4 canned pineapple rings, drained

3 tbsp wine vinegar

2 tbsp soy sauce

1½ tbsp corn oil

1 tbsp sugar

24 chicken wings

Shredded lemon zest

8 metal skewers

1 Put all the ingredients except the chicken and the lemon zest into a blender and process until smooth. Pour the mixture into a large, shallow dish. Add the chicken wings and turn until they are well coated. Cover and let stand for up to 2 hours at room temperature, or refrigerate for up to 12 hours, turning occasionally.

2 Remove the chicken wings from the marinade and thread them onto 8 skewers. Grill over medium-hot heat, occasionally brushing with the remaining marinade and turning often, until crisp and cooked through, about 20 minutes. To serve, garnish with shredded lemon zest.

Serves 6

Opposite Grilled chicken with raspberry-balsamic glaze

Sugar-spiced chicken with gingered mango

To make your chicken the authentic Cuban way, substitute blood orange or sour orange juice for the orange and lime juice. Made either way, this sweet and hot chicken tastes fantastic.

4 split chicken breasts, skinned, and flattened to a uniform thickness

FOR THE MARINADE
1/2 cup freshly squeezed orange juice
1 tbsp hot red pepper sauce
Juice of 2 limes
1/2 tsp sea salt
1/3 tsp freshly ground black pepper

FOR THE RUB
1/3 cup packed light brown sugar

1 tsp dried mustard
1 tsp allspice
1 tsp dried thyme
1/2 tsp ground cumin
1/2 tsp cayenne pepper
1/4 tsp sea salt
1/4 tsp freshly ground black pepper

FOR THE GINGERED MANGO
1 1/2 cups diced ripe mango
1/4 cup diced red onion
1 to 2 tsp shredded gingerroot
1 tsp sea salt

1 Combine the marinade ingredients and blend well. Place the chicken breasts and the marinade in a resealable plastic bag, seal, and turn to coat. Marinate in the refrigerator for 4 to 6 hours, or overnight.

2 Combine the rub ingredients in a bowl and blend. Remove the chicken from the marinade and dry a little with paper towels. Thoroughly season the chicken breasts on all sides with the rub.

3 Combine all the salsa ingredients and gently toss to combine. Cover and refrigerate until required.

4 Grill the chicken breasts over medium-hot heat, turning once, 5 to 7 minutes per side or until the juices run clear. Transfer to serving plates and serve with the gingered mango. Garnish with a lime wedge if desired.

Serves 4

Mediterranean-style poussins

This dish needs to be cooked on a covered barbecue, to ensure that the whole poussins are cooked through yet remain gloriously moist and succulent.

1/2 stick unsalted butter, softened
2 slices prosciutto, chopped finely
2 tbsp finely chopped rosemary
2 sun-dried tomatoes in oil, drained and chopped finely

2 tsp Dijon mustard
Sea salt and freshly ground black pepper to taste
2 poussins, each weighing about 1 1/4 to 1 1/2 lbs
1 small lemon

1 Put the butter, prosciutto, rosemary, tomato, and mustard into a small bowl and mix well.

2 Season the poussins lightly with salt and pepper.

3 Carefully lift the skin from the breast of each, running one or two fingers underneath to make a pocket. Spoon half the butter mixture into each pocket and smooth the skin to make a level surface.

4 Wrap each bird in oiled, heavy-duty foil, securing the seams. Grill over medium heat about 30 minutes, turning occasionally.

5 Turn the birds breast side up and, wearing oven mitts, tear open the top of each foil parcel, completely exposing the birds but holding the juices in the foil. Cover the barbecue with the lid and continue cooking another 15 minutes or until the poussins are golden brown and cooked through.

Serves 4

Opposite Mediterranean-style poussins

Lemon-herb poussins

If you can track down divine little poussins, these very young, small chickens are worth the hunt. Their meat is juicy, sweet, and delicious. Alternatively, you can use Cornish game hens.

2 tsp fresh lemon juice	black pepper
½ tsp sea salt	6 poussins
¾ stick unsalted butter	Sea salt and freshly ground
1 tbsp shredded lemon zest	black pepper
1 tsp finely chopped thyme	6 sprigs thyme
1 tsp finely chopped	2 lemons, cut into wedges
rosemary	2 tbsp melted butter
1 clove garlic, pressed	Sprigs of thyme and
¼ tsp freshly ground	rosemary, to garnish

1 Combine the lemon juice and salt, stirring to dissolve the salt, add the rest of the ingredients down to the poussins and combine until blended well.

2 Rinse the poussins in cold water and pat dry with paper towels. Season each cavity with salt and pepper. Working from the cavity end of each bird, run your fingers between the skin and the flesh of the breasts and legs to loosen the skin, being careful not to tear it. Push the lemon-herb butter under the skin and massage the skin from the outside to spread the butter evenly over the breasts and legs.

3 Insert a thyme sprig and lemon wedges into the cavity of each poussin, and then tie the legs together with twine. Brush the poussins with melted butter and season with salt and pepper.

4 Grill over medium heat, breast side down and covered, turning every 10 to 15 minutes, for 45 to 55 minutes. Transfer the poussins to a serving platter or serving plates, remove the string, and serve abundantly garnished with thyme and rosemary.

Serves 6

Grilled pheasant

If you have the chance to go pheasant hunting, be sure you know how to properly dress the meat. Pheasant skin is extremely tough and should be removed, feathers and all. If you prefer to buy your pheasant rather than catch it, you'll find it at specialty butcher shops. Serve the pheasant with a sweet, fruit-based barbecue sauce.

1 cup hard apple cider	2 tbsp finely chopped
½ cup vegetable oil	parsley
¼ cup soy sauce	2 cloves garlic, pressed
¼ cup packed dark brown	1 bay leaf
sugar	3 peppercorns
¼ cup fresh lemon juice	6 bone-in pheasant breast
2 tbsp Worcestershire sauce	halves, skin removed
2 tbsp shredded carrots	Olive oil

1 Combine all the ingredients except the pheasant in a saucepan and bring to a boil over a medium heat. Reduce heat and simmer 5 minutes. Remove from the heat and let cool to room temperature.

2 Place the pheasant in a glass baking dish. Pour the remaining marinade over the chicken, turning to make sure both sides are coated. Cover and marinate in the refrigerator for 6 to 8 hours, or overnight.

3 Remove the pheasant from the dish, reserving the remaining marinade, and pat dry with paper towels. Thoroughly brush both sides of the pheasant with olive oil and grill over medium heat, turning once and basting with the reserved marinade every 5 minutes, for 15 to 20 minutes or until the juices run clear.

Serves 6

Opposite Lemon-herb poussins

Quail halves with tequila

You might not associate quails with tequila, but this recipe will change your mind. I like serving them with fried potatoes, grilled green beans, and a salad or slaw.

1 tbsp garlic salt

2 tsp lemon pepper

1 tsp onion salt

1 tsp sugar

½ tsp celery salt

12 quail halves, breast bones removed

¼ cup good-quality gold tequila

¼ cup olive oil

1 Combine the garlic salt, lemon pepper, onion salt, sugar, and celery salt in a small bowl and blend well. Set aside.

2 Place the quail and the tequila in a resealable plastic bag, seal, and turn to coat. Marinate in the refrigerator for 1 hour.

3 Remove the quail from the tequila and pat dry with paper towels. Rub with the olive oil and thoroughly season with the spice mixture. Grill the quail over hot heat 3 to 5 minutes per side, being careful not to overcook.

Serves 4 to 6

Opposite Quail halves with tequila

Quail wrapped in grape leaves

Quail are so small that they are more of an appetizer than a main dish, so you need to cook two, or even three quail per person. This is a traditional method for cooking quail, which infuses the bird with the richness of the bacon and the smoky flavor of the grape leaves.

8 quails

Freshly ground black pepper to taste

24 slices Canadian bacon

One 16-oz can grape leaves in brine, drained and rinsed

1 Wash and dry the quail, then season generously with the black pepper. Wrap three strips of bacon around each bird, and then wrap with a grape leaf, securing with a piece of soaked twine. The birds may be prepared ahead of time, covered, and refrigerated until needed.

2 Grill the quail over medium-hot heat, turning frequently, about 15 to 20 minutes. Unless you have a large grill, you'll probably have to cook the quail in two batches.

Serves 4

Grilled quail

Be careful not to cook these delicate little birds for too long, or they'll get tough. When cooked just right, they are truly succulent.

1 tbsp minced garlic

Juice of 1 lemon

¼ cup dry vermouth

1 tbsp juniper berries, smashed

½ tsp dried thyme leaves

2 tsp rubbed sage

Salt and pepper to taste

2 tbsp olive oil

Six 4 to 5 oz quails, split open at the backbone to lie flat

1 Combine all the ingredients except the quail and mix well.

2 Place the quail in a glass baking dish. Pour the marinade over the quail, turning to make sure both sides are coated. Cover and refrigerate for 1 to 4 hours, or overnight.

3 Grill over medium-hot heat, skin side down, for 8 to 10 minutes. Turn and cook about 5 to 6 minutes more or until the juices run clear.

Serves 6

Cornish game hens with lemon-cilantro marinade

When I prepare these birds for guests, I often pair them with wild rice pilaf and some greens. For some people, half a bird is just enough, but for big eaters like me, I serve one whole hen per person.

Two 24-oz Cornish game hens, halved (ask your butcher to do this)	3 tbsp finely chopped cilantro
2 tsp ground coriander	2 cloves garlic, pressed
1 tsp ground turmeric	2 whole scallions, sliced thinly
½ cup fresh lemon juice	2 tbsp garlic salt
¼ cup olive oil	2 tsp freshly ground black pepper

1 Rinse the hens with cold water and pat dry with paper towels. Combine the coriander and turmeric, blend well, and rub the hens with the mixture. Set aside.

2 Combine the remaining ingredients, except the garlic salt and pepper, in a medium bowl.

3 Place the hens in a large glass baking dish. Pour the marinade over the hens, turning to make sure all sides are coated. Cover and marinate in the refrigerator for 4 to 6 hours, or overnight.

4 Remove the hens, reserving the marinade, and blot dry with paper towels. Season with garlic salt and pepper. Grill over medium-hot heat, starting skin side down, turning and basting occasionally with the reserved marinade, for 20 to 25 minutes or until the juices run clear.

Serves 2 to 4

Grilled venison steaks

People often make the mistake of overcooking venison and other game. At the most, it should be cooked to medium, or better yet, medium-rare.

½ cup Italian salad dressing	Sea salt and freshly ground black pepper
½ cup soy sauce	
2 tbsp A.1. Steak Sauce or spicy mustard	2 venison steaks, ½-inch thick
1 tbsp Worcestershire sauce	
2 cloves garlic, pressed	

1 Combine all the marinade ingredients and blend well. Place the steaks and the marinade in a resealable plastic bag, seal, and turn to coat. Marinate in the refrigerator for 2 to 4 hours.

2 Grill the venison over hot heat for 3 to 4 minutes per side, just enough to leave some pink in the middle.

Serves 4

Opposite Grilled venison steaks

Barbecued duck breasts and porcini mushrooms

The southwest of France is known for its dishes made with duck, as well as for its abundance of fungi, which are usually eaten together in simple dishes such as this. Begin the meal with a robust vegetable soup, drink a delicious Paulliac or Gaillac, and follow with a plate of delectable French cheeses.

4 boned duck breasts, skin on

Sea salt and freshly ground black pepper to taste

¼ cup red wine

5 cloves garlic, chopped

3 tbsp olive oil

1½ lbs porcini mushrooms, or other large mushrooms

2 tbsp chopped parsley

1 Score the skin of the duck evenly, then place in a bowl. Toss with the salt, pepper, and half the wine, half the garlic, and half the oil. Marinate for at least one hour.

2 Toss the mushrooms with the remaining wine, garlic, and oil, and some salt and pepper. These do not need to marinate longer than a few minutes.

3 Grill the duck breasts over hot heat, starting skin side down, about 5 minutes on the skin side, and 2 to 3 minutes on the flesh side for medium-rare. As the fat melts and drips off the duck, the skin will become crispy. Meanwhile, grill the mushrooms over hot heat, a few minutes per side.

4 Thinly slice the duck across the grain and serve with the mushrooms and a sprinkling of parsley.

Serves 4

Duck breast with gingery balsamic-orange sauce

Duck – whether wild or domestic – is delicious, and tastes best when cooked to medium-rare. This sauce is a perfect complement for the flavorful grilled duck.

1 large duck breast, skinned

½ cup fresh orange juice

1½ cups chicken stock

¼ cup balsamic vinegar

2 tsp shredded gingerroot

½ stick unsalted butter

½ tsp sea salt

1 tsp freshly ground black pepper

1 tsp orange zest

2 tbsp vegetable oil

3 oranges, sliced thickly

1 Rinse the duck and pat dry with paper towels. Set aside.

2 Combine the orange juice and chicken stock in a pan over medium-high heat. Bring to a boil and, uncovered, reduce by half, which will take about 15 to 20 minutes. Add the balsamic vinegar and ginger and cook for 2 to 3 minutes more. While constantly whisking, add the butter, 1 tablespoon at a time. After the butter is completely incorporated, add the salt, pepper, and zest.

3 Brush the duck breast with the oil. Grill over hot heat. For medium-rare duck, grill 5 to 8 minutes per side, or until the doneness you desire. Grill the orange slices until they soften and char slightly.

4 Serve the duck on a bed of griddled orange slices, with the sauce poured over.

Serves 2 to 4

Opposite Duck breast with gingery balsamic-orange sauce

Cajun duck with sour cream dressing

Sour cream is a perfect foil for the spiciness of these exciting Cajun seasonings.

4 duck breasts, skinless

3 tbsp olive oil

2 cloves garlic, chopped finely

2 small celery stalks, chopped finely

1 tbsp ground coriander

1 tbsp dried mixed herbs

1½ tsp ground cumin

1 tsp chili powder

1 tsp sugar

Sea salt and freshly ground black pepper to taste

1½ cups sour cream

4 tbsp snipped fresh chives or chopped cilantro

1 Put each duck breast between two sheets of plastic wrap. Using a rolling pin, beat and flatten the duck breasts until they are about twice the original size. Lay them in a large glass baking dish.

2 Put the remaining ingredients, except the sour cream and chives, into a blender or food processor and blend until smooth. Pour the mixture over the duck, turning to make sure all sides are coated. Cover and marinate at room temperature for 2 hours, or longer if refrigerated, turning occasionally.

3 Combine the sour cream and chives in a small bowl and mix well. Cover and chill until needed.

4 Transfer the duck to the barbecue and cook over high heat until slightly charred and just cooked through, 2 to 3 minutes per side. Serve immediately with the sour cream mixture.

Serves 4

Duck and apricot skewers

The hearty, sweet flavor of duck is deliciously partnered with the slight acidity of fresh apricots. Make sure the fruit is not overripe, or it will disintegrate during cooking.

4 duck breasts (about 2 lbs total)

8 firm-ripe fresh apricots

4 tbsp light soy sauce

4 tbsp orange marmalade

Freshly ground black pepper to taste

8 flat metal skewers

1 If necessary, remove the skin from the duck. Cut into chunks and place in a glass baking dish. Halve the apricots and remove their pits.

2 Combine the soy sauce, marmalade, and pepper in a small bowl and mix well. Pour the marinade over the duck, cover, and marinate at room temperature for 2 hours, or longer in the refrigerator, stirring occasionally.

3 Thread the duck and apricots alternately on to flat metal skewers. Grill over medium-high heat, turning occasionally, 8 to 10 minutes, or to the doneness you desire.

Serves 4

Opposite Cajun duck with sour cream dressing

Black Forest turkey sandwich

This filling sandwich is good for all sorts of outdoor eating, from a barbecue on the patio to a picnic in the park. Try serving it with German potato salad and a good lager beer.

2 tbsp vegetable oil

½ lb shredded red cabbage

2 tart apples, peeled, cored, and chopped

2 tbsp onion salt

1 tsp ground cinnamon

1 tsp freshly ground black pepper

Six 4 to 5 oz turkey breasts

12 slices black rye or pumpernickel bread

6 slices Swiss cheese

¼ cup mayonnaise

¼ cup coarse ground mustard

Olive oil

1 Heat the oil in a large skillet and add the cabbage and apples. Cook until wilted and tender, about 7 to 10 minutes. Drain well and keep warm.

2 Combine the onion salt, cinnamon, and pepper in a small bowl and blend well. In a separate bowl, combine the mayonnaise and mustard and blend well.

3 Season the turkey breasts on both sides with the seasoning mixture and brush them with olive oil. Grill over medium-hot heat for 4 to 5 minutes per side.

4 To serve, spread the mustard mixture on each slice of bread, and add some cabbage mixture, a turkey breast, a slice of cheese, and top with another slice of bread. Cut each sandwich in half and serve.

Serves 6

Turkey yakitori

These delicious, tender kabobs can be served hot or cold. When skewering the meat, do not push the pieces too close together or the turkey will take longer to cook. Serve with shredded daikon radish topped with a splash of rice vinegar, and a salad.

FOR THE TURKEY

1 lb turkey breast

2 tbsp sake or sherry

2 tbsp light soy sauce

1 tbsp dark soy sauce

2 tbsp orange juice

1 tbsp packed brown sugar

8 wooden skewers, soaked

Olive oil

Scallions and cucumber, to garnish

FOR THE DIPPING SAUCE

2 tbsp light soy sauce

4 tbsp orange juice

2 scallions, trimmed and chopped finely

1 small chile, seeded and chopped finely

1 Cut the turkey into thin strips and place in a glass baking dish. Combine the sake, soy sauces, orange juice, and brown sugar in a small bowl and mix well. Pour the marinade over the turkey, stirring to be sure all the pieces are coated. Cover and marinate in the refrigerator for 30 minutes, stirring occasionally.

2 Drain the turkey and thread the meat onto eight small wooden skewers.

3 Meanwhile, combine all the dipping sauce ingredients in a small bowl and mix well. Set aside to allow the flavors to blend.

4 Lightly brush the turkey skewers with olive oil. Grill over medium heat, turning frequently, 8 to 10 minutes.

5 Garnish with sliced scallions and cucumber and serve with the dipping sauce.

Serves 4

Above left Black Forest turkey sandwich **right** Turkey yakitori

Spicy-marmalade turkey cutlets

Canned pineapple slices may be substituted – use as many drained rings as you like – but if you're using a fresh pineapple, save the leafy top to use as a garnish for the center of your serving platter. Serve with a hot or cold rice dish.

1 medium pineapple, cut lengthwise into quarters with the rind on, and then scored crosswise into 1-inch thick slices

1 orange, cut into $\frac{1}{2}$-inch slices

$1\frac{1}{2}$ tbsp packed light brown sugar

8 oz marmalade

2 tbsp finely chopped scallions (white and green parts)

$\frac{1}{2}$ tsp pressed garlic

$\frac{1}{2}$ tsp red pepper sauce

$\frac{1}{4}$ tsp shredded gingerroot

$\frac{1}{2}$ tbsp Worcestershire sauce

$\frac{1}{2}$ tbsp vegetable oil

Sea salt and freshly ground black pepper to taste

Four $\frac{1}{2}$-inch thick turkey cutlets

1 Sprinkle the pineapple and orange slices with the brown sugar.

2 Combine the marmalade, scallions, garlic, red pepper sauce, ginger, Worcestershire sauce, oil, salt, and pepper in a small bowl and mix well.

3 Grill the turkey cutlets and fruit over medium heat, brushing the turkey frequently with the marmalade mixture, turning the turkey and fruit occasionally, about 5 to 7 minutes or until the turkey just loses its pink color. Serve.

Serves 4

Apple wood-grilled turkey tenderloins

Apple wood on the grill really makes this dish special. It adds an extra smoky sweetness to the natural grill flavors. Beforehand, check that your grill is appropriate for use with wood chips by referring to the manufacturer's instruction manual.

1 cup apple wood chips, soaked in water

2 tbsp garlic salt

1 tsp freshly ground black pepper

2 lbs turkey tenderloins

Olive oil

1 Combine the garlic salt and pepper, blend well, and thoroughly season the tenderloins with the mixture. Brush the tenderloins on all sides with olive oil.

2 Add the wood chips to a medium-hot grill. Grill the tenderloins, covered with the grill lid, turning once, for 8 to 9 minutes per side.

3 Remove from the grill and let rest for about 5 to 10 minutes before slicing into $\frac{1}{2}$-inch thick medallions to serve.

Serves 4 to 6

The perfect hamburger

These burgers must of course be served with lettuce, grilled red peppers, mustard, mayonnaise, tomato, relish, and ketchup. And don't forget the fries.

1 lb ground beef	**Sea salt and freshly ground**
3 shallots, peeled and	**black pepper to taste**
chopped finely	**4 hamburger buns**
1 to 2 tsp horseradish sauce	
2 tbsp chopped fresh parsley	

1 Combine all the ingredients except the buns in a large bowl, mixing with slightly wet hands. Form into four burgers.

2 Grill the burgers over medium heat, 4 to 6 minutes per side or until the doneness you desire.

3 Meanwhile, split the buns and place them, cut side down, on the grill until toasted. Serve the burgers on the buns, lavishly accompanied with the essential ingredients listed above. Simply perfect.

Serves 4

Barbecued Texan T-bone steaks

For most of us, this recipe would feed a family of four, but in Texas, where out-sized appetites are the norm, it will be enough to satisfy two people! Serve with grilled potatoes and asparagus.

2 thick T-bone steaks	**1 tbsp Dijon mustard**
(about 3 lbs)	**1 tsp Worcestershire sauce**
¼ cup balsamic vinegar	**½ tsp fresh lime juice**
2 cloves garlic, halved	**Sea salt and freshly ground**
1 tbsp coarsely ground	**black pepper to taste**
black pepper	
½ stick unsalted butter,	
softened	

1 Trim the fat from around the steaks.

2 Using a pastry brush, thoroughly coat each steak on both sides with the balsamic vinegar. Rub half a clove of garlic all over both sides of each steak. Season with coarse black pepper, pressing it into the meat. Cover and set aside.

3 Combine the remaining ingredients except the salt and pepper in a small bowl and blend well.

4 Using a pastry brush, brush the sauce all over the steaks. Grill the steaks over medium heat, basting with the sauce after turning, 8 to 10 minutes per side, or longer if you desire. Serve on a warm platter with extra sauce on the side.

Serves 4 to 6

Opposite The perfect hamburger

"Killer" barbecued flank steak

I've enjoyed this flank steak recipe more times than I can remember, and I'm convinced it gets better each time.

¼ cup Worcestershire sauce

¼ cup olive oil

2 tbsp bottled steak sauce

4 cloves garlic, pressed

2 tsp fresh lemon juice

1 tsp hot pepper sauce

½ tsp dried mustard

½ cup finely chopped cilantro

½ cup finely chopped parsley

One 1½ to 2 lb flank steak

1 Combine all the marinade ingredients except the flank steak and blend well.

2 Trim the meat of all unwanted fat and place in a glass dish. Pour in the marinade. Add the steak to the marinade, coating both sides. Cover and marinate in the refrigerator for 24 hours, turning the meat 4 to 6 times.

3 One hour before cooking, remove the flank steak from the marinade and pat dry with paper towels, reserving the marinade.

4 Grill the steaks over hot heat to the desired doneness, basting with the reserved marinade as they cook. For medium, grill for 7 to 8 minutes each side; for well done, 10 minutes will be required. To serve, slice on the bias and across the grain.

Serves 4 to 6

Right Flank steak with rosemary-orange glaze

Flank steak with rosemary-orange glaze

Always remember that when grilling flank steak, you don't want to overcook it. It is tough to start with, which is why it benefits from being marinated overnight. Lightly cooking the meat will help with its tenderness.

1 cup teriyaki sauce

½ cup fresh orange juice

½ cup finely chopped onions

4 cloves garlic, pressed

1 scallion, thinly sliced (green and white parts)

⅓ cup corn syrup

2 tbsp packed dark brown sugar

2 tbsp chopped rosemary

1 tbsp toasted sesame oil

2 tsp sesame seeds

1 tsp crushed red pepper

One 1 to 2 lb flank steak

1 Combine all the ingredients except the steak in a medium bowl and blend well.

2 Trim the meat of all unwanted fat and place in a glass baking dish. Pour the marinade over the steak, turning to make sure all sides are coated. Cover and marinate in the refrigerator for 24 hours, turning the meat 4 to 6 times.

3 One hour before cooking, remove the flank steak from the marinade and pat dry with paper towels, reserving the marinade.

4 Grill the steak over hot heat to the doneness you desire, basting with the reserved marinade to create a sweet glaze.

5 To serve, slice on the bias, across the grain. Place the remaining marinade in a saucepan and bring to a boil, and reduce to concentrate the flavors. Serve poured over the sliced meat.

Serves 4 to 6

Flatiron steaks with North African marinade

Flatiron steak is another name for chuck steak. It is a very tasty cut of beef, and this North African marinade makes it even better.

1 Spanish onion, chopped finely

2 tbsp shredded gingerroot

4 cloves garlic, pressed

½ cup olive oil

⅓ cup fresh lemon juice

¼ cup finely chopped cilantro

2 tbsp soy sauce

1 tbsp dry sherry

1 tbsp chili powder

2 tsp harrissa or other hot sauce (optional)

2 tsp sea salt

1 tsp ground turmeric

1 tsp ground marjoram

1 tsp freshly ground black pepper

4 flatiron steaks (chuck steak) (6 to 8 oz each)

1 Combine all the ingredients except the steak in a medium bowl and mix well.

2 With a sharp fork, pierce the steaks all over and on both sides. Place the steaks in a resealable plastic bag or shallow glass baking dish, add the marinade, and turn to coat. Cover and marinate in the refrigerator overnight, turning the meat occasionally.

3 Before cooking, let the steaks come to room temperature. Because these steaks are somewhat firm and chewy to start with, it is recommended they be cooked medium to medium-rare. Grill over medium-hot heat, 8 to 10 minutes per side. Let the steaks rest, covered loosely with foil, for 5 minutes before serving.

Serves 4

Thai beef kabobs

Remember when using fresh chiles that the heat is not only in the seeds, but also in the membrane to which they are attached. Do not touch any sensitive parts of the body until you have thoroughly washed your hands. To be safe, wear rubber gloves when handling chiles.

FOR THE DIPPING SAUCE

3 tbsp light soy sauce

1 tbsp mirin (sweet rice wine) or sherry

1 Thai chile, seeded and chopped finely

2 scallions (white and green parts), trimmed and chopped finely

FOR THE KABOBS

1 lb sirloin steak

1 tbsp shredded gingerroot

2 stalks lemongrass, outer leaves removed and chopped

1 to 2 Thai chiles, seeded if preferred, and chopped

3 cloves garlic, pressed

4 tbsp fresh lime juice

2 tbsp vegetable oil

2 tbsp chopped cilantro

8 wooden skewers, soaked

1 Combine the dipping sauce ingredients and set aside to allow the flavors to blend.

2 Trim the steak, cut into long thin strips, and place in a glass baking dish. Scatter with the ginger, lemongrass, chile, and garlic. Blend the lime juice and oil and pour over the steak. Cover loosely and marinate in the refrigerator for 30 minutes.

3 Drain the steak and thread onto the skewers. Lightly brush the rack with oil, and grill the steak on medium heat for 2 to 4 minutes per side, or to the doneness you desire.

4 Serve sprinkled with the cilantro and accompany with the dipping sauce.

Serves 4

Above left Flatiron steaks with North African marinade **right** Thai beef kabobs

California tri-tip

Tri-tip is generally considered a California treat. It uses a special cut of beef, the triangular-shaped, boneless, bottom sirloin butt can be purchased from any knowledgeable butcher. In fact, you can give your butcher the product code from the Meat Buyers Guide (Item 185 C & 185 D). Sirloin steak can be substituted in this recipe, but in my opinion, it's not as good.

1 tri-tip (bottom sirloin)
   3 to 6 lbs, trimmed

FOR THE SALSA

One 48-oz can crushed
   tomatoes

1 medium onion, diced

½ cup chopped cilantro

2 cloves garlic, minced

2 fresh jalapeño peppers,
   seeded and chopped finely

1 tsp ground cumin

Sea salt and freshly ground
   black pepper

FOR THE RUB

3 tbsp packed light
   brown sugar

2 tbsp salt

2 tbsp coarsely ground
   black pepper

2 tbsp granulated garlic

2 tbsp sweet Hungarian
   paprika

2 tbsp parsley flakes

2 tbsp granulated onion

1 tsp ground cumin

1 tsp cayenne pepper

1 Combine all the salsa ingredients in a medium bowl and blend well. Refrigerate until needed.

2 Combine all the rub ingredients in a small bowl and blend well.

3 Thoroughly season the tri-tip on all sides with the rub.

4 Grill over medium-hot heat for 10 minutes, turn, and cook another 10 minutes, repeating the process until the internal temperature reaches 130°F. Cook longer if desired. To serve, slice the meat thinly across the grain. Top with the salsa.

Serves 6 to 12

Korean beef

In Korea, this dish would be served with kimchi (pickled salty cabbage), stir-fried bean sprouts, and plain rice. If you can't get kimchi, try a coleslaw or cucumber salad with a vinegar dressing.

1 tbsp sesame seeds

1 cup finely chopped
   scallions (white and green
   parts)

2 to 4 cloves garlic, finely
   chopped

¼ cup soy sauce

2 tbsp sugar

2 tbsp dry sherry or sake

2 tbsp peanut or sesame oil

1½ lbs beef, such as chuck,
   round, or sirloin

1 Toast the sesame seeds in a heavy skillet, shaking frequently to avoid burning and popping, until golden. Grind the toasted seeds in a mortar and pestle or spice grinder.

2 Combine the ground sesame seeds with the scallions, garlic, soy sauce, sugar, sherry, and oil in a small bowl and mix well.

3 Slice the meat into strips about ¼-inch thick. Place the meat in a glass baking dish. Pour the marinade over the beef, stirring to make sure the pieces are well coated. Marinate for 1 to 2 hours, covered, in the refrigerator.

4 Grill the beef over high heat until browned, but still rare, about 30 seconds to 1 minute per side.

Serves 4 to 6

Sirloin steak with pineapple chutney

With its fruity content in the relish that is served with the steak, this recipe has strong Caribbean connections.

2 lbs sirloin steak, trimmed of fat

3 tbsp vegetable oil

FOR THE RUB

Sea salt and freshly ground black pepper

1 tsp curry powder

¼ tsp garlic powder

¼ tsp ground ginger

½ tsp allspice

Dash of nutmeg

Dash of cinnamon

FOR THE CHUTNEY

20-oz can crushed pineapple, drained

¼ cup finely chopped scallions (white and green parts)

¼ cup flaked coconut, preferably unsweetened

⅓ cup finely chopped red bell pepper

1 tbsp red pepper sauce

1 tbsp shredded gingerroot

1 tbsp fresh lime juice

1 tbsp dark rum

Sea salt and white pepper to taste

1 Combine the rub ingredients in a small bowl and mix well. Transfer the rub to a large sheet of waxed paper.

2 Brush both sides of the steak with the oil and roll the steak in it, patting the seasoning into the meat. Set aside.

3 For the chutney, combine all the ingredients in a glass bowl and gently toss. Cover and let stand at room temperature until needed

4 Brush the rack with oil and grill the steak over hot heat, about 8 minutes per side for medium-rare, or to the doneness you desire. Transfer to a serving platter and serve with the chutney.

Serves 4 to 6

Japanese-style beef skewer

A *hibachi* is required here to capture the full Japanese style. No *hibachi*? Use an ordinary barbecue!

1 cup sesame seeds

2 tsp peanut oil

½ cup Japanese soy sauce

2 tbsp mirin (sweet rice wine)

1 tbsp superfine sugar

1 tbsp instant *dashi* powder

½ cup warm water

1½ lbs sirloin steak

4 sticks preserved ginger, sliced

2 scallions (white and green parts), sliced thinly

8 to 12 metal skewers

1 Dry roast the sesame seeds in a heavy skillet over medium heat until the seeds are golden brown, being careful not to burn.

2 Place the roasted sesame seeds and the oil in a blender or food processor and blend until a smooth paste is formed.

3 Mix the paste with the soy sauce, mirin, sugar, *dashi* powder, and warm water in a small bowl. Cover and refrigerate before use.

4 Cut the beef into 1-inch cubes and place in a glass baking dish. Stir the marinade, and then add it to the meat, stirring to make sure all the pieces are well coated. Cover and marinate in the refrigerator overnight.

5 Remove the beef from dish, reserving the marinade, and thread onto skewers, inserting two slices of preserved ginger between every two cubes of meat.

6 Brush the meat with the reserved marinade and grill over hot heat, about 10 minutes. Continue to brush with the marinade during cooking.

7 To serve, place the skewers on a serving dish and sprinkle with the scallion.

Serves 4 to 6

Rib-eye steaks with apple-horseradish sauce

This apple-horseradish sauce is a good accompaniment for grilled beef and prime rib. The creaminess of the sour cream in combination with the apple and horseradish makes for a uniquely flavorful sauce.

Four 10 to 12 oz rib-eye steaks

¼ cup Worcestershire sauce

FOR THE SAUCE

1 apple, peeled, cored, and shredded

½ cup sour cream or plain yogurt

¼ cup fresh horseradish

4 beef bouillon cubes

1 clove garlic, pressed

FOR THE HERB RUB

Salt and freshly ground black pepper

½ tsp dried thyme

½ tsp dried savory

½ tsp dried marjoram

½ tsp rubbed sage

¼ tsp ground bay leaf

1 Combine all the sauce ingredients in a small bowl and blend well. Set aside.

2 Combine all the herb rub ingredients in a small bowl and blend well.

3 Coat the steaks with the Worcestershire sauce and thoroughly season with the herb rub. Cover and let rest 1 to 2 hours.

4 Grill the steaks over medium-hot heat, 7 to 8 minutes per side for medium-rare. Or, cook to the doneness you desire. Serve with the apple-horseradish sauce.

Serves 4 to 6

Right Glazed rib-eye steaks with smoky corn salsa

Glazed rib-eye steaks with smoky corn salsa

These rib-eye steaks are deceptively simple to prepare and will spice up your evening. Don't forget the steak knife!

Six 1-inch thick rib-eye steaks

Sea salt and freshly ground black pepper

FOR THE SALSA

3 ears fresh corn, husked

½ cup diced red bell pepper

¼ cup thinly sliced scallions (white and green parts)

¼ cup diced red onion

Juice of 2 limes

2 tbsp jalapeño jelly, or raspberry jelly

1 tsp chili powder

1 tsp sea salt

½ tsp cumin seeds, toasted and ground

1 serrano chile, seeded and chopped finely

FOR THE SAUCE

½ cup jalapeño jelly, or raspberry jelly

½ cup ketchup

1 For the salsa, grill the ears of corn quickly over medium-hot heat, turning so they cook and color evenly, darkening without turning black. When cool enough to handle, cut the kernels from the ears and place in a medium bowl. Add the red pepper, onions, and lime, and gently toss to combine.

2 Combine the jalapeño jelly with the chili powder, salt, cumin, and serrano chile in a separate bowl and whisk to blend. Add the mixture to the vegetables and gently toss to mix. Set aside.

3 For the sauce, combine the jalapeño jelly and ketchup in a small pan and simmer 10 to 12 minutes or until the ingredients are incorporated. Set aside.

4 Season the steaks on both sides with the garlic salt and pepper. Grill over medium-hot heat, glazing the steaks with the sauce as you turn them, 5 to 7 minutes per side for medium-rare, or longer if desired. Transfer to plates and serve with the corn salsa.

Serves 6

Lamb chops with Israeli pepper relish

This relish, or salad, from Israel is known as *Horef*, and is made with mixed sweet and hot peppers, tomatoes, and spices.

Four ¾-inch thick lamb loin chops

5 tbsp olive oil

2 green bell peppers, cut into thick slices

2 mild green chiles, sliced

2 to 3 green chiles, sliced

5 to 7 cloves garlic, chopped

1¼ lbs tomatoes, diced, or one 14-oz can crushed tomatoes

1 tsp curry powder

Seeds from 2 to 3

cardamom pods or a pinch ground cardamom

Pinch of ground cumin

Pinch of ground turmeric

Pinch of ground ginger

Pinch of sugar or to taste

Salt and freshly ground black pepper to taste

Juice of ½ lemon, or to taste

1 For the relish, heat the oil in a skillet and sauté the peppers, both types of chiles, and garlic until softened, then add the tomato, curry powder, and remaining spices except the sugar, salt, and pepper. Continue to cook until the mixture thickens.

2 Season with the sugar, salt, and pepper, and add the lemon juice. Remove from the heat and chill until needed.

3 Grill the lamb chops over hot heat, 4 to 5 minutes per side. Serve topped with the pepper relish.

Serves 4

Grilled butterflied leg of lamb

You just might see me enter this recipe into the National Lamb Barbecue Contest which is held in Bonner Springs, Kansas each September. People come from around the world to share their best grilled lamb recipes.

One 5 to 7 lb leg spring lamb, deboned and butterflied (ask your butcher to do this)

8 cloves garlic, sliced thinly

4 tbsp finely chopped rosemary

1 tbsp sea salt

¼ cup olive oil

Juice of 2 lemons

2 tsp freshly ground black pepper

3 sprigs fresh rosemary

1 Combine all the ingredients except the lamb in a small bowl.

2 Rub the marinade all over the lamb. Place in a glass baking dish or resealable plastic bag and let the lamb marinate in the refrigerator for 2 to 4 hours, or overnight.

3 Remove the lamb from the refrigerator 30 minutes before grilling.

4 Begin grilling over hot heat to sear the lamb, 5 to 7 minutes per side. Depending upon the type of grill you are using, either turn the grill down to medium-hot, or spread out the coals so your fire cools to medium-hot. Grill the lamb for 30 to 40 minutes, covered if your grill has a lid, turning often. For medium-rare, cook until the internal temperature reaches 130°F to 135°F. Or, cook to the doneness you desire. Serve with fresh rosemary sprigs as garnish.

Serves 8 to 10

Opposite Grilled butterflied leg of lamb

Crispy lamb ribs

Although lamb is growing in popularity, you may have difficulty finding whole breasts of lamb in the supermarket. Instead, you can ask your butcher for lamb riblets, which are the breasts of lamb already cut into individual pieces.

**2 breasts of lamb
(about 3 lbs)**

**Shredded zest and juice
1 lemon**

2 cloves garlic, pressed

2 tsp dried marjoram

2 tsp tomato paste

1 tsp packed brown sugar

Pinch cayenne pepper

¼ tsp sea salt

2 tbsp water

1 Trim large areas of fat off the lamb. Cut the breast into ribs (or pairs of ribs). Alternatively, ask the butcher to cut the meat up for you. Place the ribs in a bowl.

2 Mix the remaining ingredients. Pour the marinade over the ribs, turning to make sure they are well coated. Cover and marinate in the refrigerator for 2 to 4 hours.

3 Grill the lamb over medium heat, covered, turning frequently, 10 to 15 minutes, or until well browned.

Serves 4

Right Café la Paz lamb sausage

Café la Paz lamb sausage

For those who have never made sausage, I recommend trying it. Sausage is really nothing more than seasoned chopped meat. This particular sausage has a character all its own, and a great sounding name with no meaning – I just liked the sound of it! If you like lamb, you will certainly enjoy this dish. Accompany it with sweet potato mash.

3 lbs ground lamb

2 tbsp olive oil

2 tbsp sweet Hungarian paprika

1 tbsp sea salt

2 tsp ground cumin, toasted

2 tsp ground coriander, toasted

1 tsp granulated garlic

1 tsp crushed red pepper

1 tsp lemon zest

1 tsp fennel seeds

½ tsp freshly ground black pepper

¼ cup red wine

3 tbsp finely chopped cilantro, to garnish

1 Combine all the ingredients in a large bowl and blend well, working the mixture until it gets sticky.

2 With clean, cool hands, form the mixture into patties or roll into a loaf or log. Sausage is best the day after you make it, so refrigerate for 24 hours.

3 Grill over medium heat, 5 to 7 minutes per side, or until done. Serve garnished with chopped cilantro.

Serves 4 to 6

Loin of lamb with walnut-onion chutney

This is a cross between a traditional chutney and an onion marmalade, and combines the crunch of nuts with a fruity onion base. This cut of lamb is special when served with the chutney.

2¼ lbs onions, sliced thinly

4 tbsp olive oil

1 lb apples, peeled, cored, and chopped

1 cup red wine

1 cup sugar

Sea salt and freshly ground black pepper

⅓ cup red wine vinegar

2 cups chopped walnuts

Fresh lemon juice to taste

3 lbs boneless loin of lamb

1 For the walnut-onion chutney, heat the oil in a large, deep skillet and cook the onions until well softened, about 10 minutes.

2 Add the apples and red wine and simmer until both the onions and apples are well cooked, about 20 minutes.

3 Stir in the sugar, salt, pepper, and vinegar and cook for another 30 minutes until the chutney is thickened and most of the liquid has been absorbed.

4 Add the walnuts and lemon juice and stir them evenly throughout the mixture. Continue cooking for another 10 minutes until all the liquid has gone. Remove from the heat and set aside.

5 Grill the lamb over medium heat, covered, 25 minutes per pound for well done or 22 minutes per pound for medium, or until the internal temperature reaches 170°F for well-done, 160°F for medium. Serve with the walnut-onion chutney. The leftover chutney can be kept refrigerated in an airtight container for 3 to 4 weeks.

Serves 4 to 6

Green peppercorn and mustard lamb steaks

A spicy mustard paste is spread thickly over the lamb steaks, giving them a real flavor lift.

1 tbsp green peppercorns, chopped finely

4 tbsp whole-grain mustard

3 tbsp chopped scallions (white and green parts)

½ cup fresh bread crumbs

3 tbsp chopped fresh parsley

¼ tsp cayenne pepper

1 to 1½ tbsp vegetable oil

Four 1-inch thick lamb steaks

1 Put the peppercorns, mustard, scallions, bread crumbs, parsley, and cayenne pepper in a bowl and mix well. Stir in a bit of oil at a time, just enough to help make a thick paste.

2 Spread the paste on both sides of the lamb steaks and place in a glass baking dish. Cover and marinate at room temperature for 2 hours, or refrigerate for up to 24 hours.

3 Grill the lamb steaks over medium heat 6 to 8 minutes per side, or to the doneness you desire.

Serves 4

Opposite Green peppercorn and mustard lamb steaks

Skewered lamb with red currant coulis

Lamb and red currants are a delicious combination of flavors. Red currants are only in season for a short time, so it's worth freezing some when they are available, to use out of season.

1 lb lean lamb, such as leg, sirloin chops, cubed

2 tbsp red currant jelly

3 tbsp raspberry vinegar

2 tsp soy sauce

2 tbsp vegetable oil

8 fresh rosemary sprigs or wooden skewers, soaked

FOR THE COULIS

2/3 cup fresh red currants, rinsed

2 to 3 sprigs fresh mint

1 to 2 tbsp packed brown sugar, or to taste

1 tbsp raspberry vinegar

1 Place the cubed lamb in a glass baking dish. Heat the red currant jelly with the vinegar, soy sauce, and oil and stir until blended. Pour the marinade over the lamb, stirring to be sure the pieces are well coated. Cover and refrigerate 30 minutes, occasionally spooning the marinade over the lamb.

2 Shred the leaves from the bottom of the sprigs of rosemary, and when ready to cook, drain the lamb and thread onto the rosemary sprigs. Alternatively, use wooden skewers.

3 Meanwhile, make the coulis by cooking the red currants with the mint sprigs, brown sugar, and vinegar over medium-low heat. Simmer for 10 minutes or until tender. Pass through a fine sieve to form a smooth sauce. Set aside.

4 Grill the lamb skewers over medium heat, 3 to 5 minutes per side or to the doneness you desire. Serve with the coulis.

Serves 4

Lamb burgers with curried cucumber

If you like regular hamburgers, then you will really like lamb burgers. The curried cucumber brings alive the flavors in the lamb. As a variation, try using a combination of ground lamb and ground beef.

FOR THE CURRIED CUCUMBER

1 cucumber, halved lengthwise, seeded and sliced thinly

1/3 cup plain yogurt

2 tsp fresh lemon juice

2 tsp honey

1/2 to 1 tsp curry powder

Sea salt and freshly ground black pepper

FOR THE BURGERS

1 1/2 lbs ground lamb

2 tsp salt

1 tsp freshly ground black pepper

4 wedges focaccia bread

2 tbsp olive oil

1 red leaf lettuce

1 For the curried cucumber, combine all the ingredients except the cucumber and mix well. Add the dressing to the cucumber and gently mix. Set aside until needed.

2 Place the lamb in a bowl and season with the salt and pepper.

3 Form into four burgers each about 1-inch thick. Grill the burgers over medium-hot heat, 5 to 7 minutes per side for medium-rare, or longer if desired.

4 Meanwhile, split the focaccia wedges in half and brush with oil. Toast on the grill while the burgers are cooking until the bread is golden brown, about 35 to 45 seconds.

5 To assemble, top each half of bread with a burger, lettuce leaves, some curried cucumber, and another piece of bread. Serve hot.

Serves 4

Above left Skewered lamb with red currant coulis **right** Lamb burgers with curried cucumber

Small spicy Moorish kabobs

Kabobs of one kind or another are eaten and enjoyed all over the world. Almost every culture has a version of skewered meat cooked over a fire.

2 cloves garlic, chopped finely	Freshly ground black pepper
2 tsp sea salt	3 tbsp olive oil
1 tsp curry powder	1 tbsp fresh lemon juice
1/2 tsp coriander seeds	1 lb lean pork, cut into small cubes
1 tsp paprika	6 bamboo skewers, soaked
1/4 tsp dried thyme	Lime wedges

1 Crush the chopped garlic with the salt using a mortar and pestle.

2 Work the curry powder, coriander seeds, paprika, thyme, black pepper, oil, and lemon juice into the garlic and salt. Transfer to a shallow dish and set aside.

3 Remove any excess fat from the pork and chop into small, bite-sized cubes. Skewer the meat, three to four cubes to a stick, and turn the kabobs in the marinade to thoroughly coat. Let marinate for a few hours – the longer you leave them, the better the flavor.

4 Cook over high heat until the meat is browned on the outside and cooked through, about 3 to 5 minutes each side, 12 to 20 minutes in total.

5 Serve immediately with lime wedges.

Serves 3 to 4

Indonesian pork brochettes

Coconut, ginger, chiles, and lime give a distinctly Asian flavor to these pork skewers. You could use cubes of chicken or shrimp instead if you prefer.

1 cup coconut milk	Salt and freshly ground black pepper
6 scallions (white and green parts)	Generous pinch of ground turmeric
2 cloves garlic	1 3/4 lbs lean pork, cubed
2 fresh red chiles, halved and seeded	Six metal skewers
2-inch piece gingerroot, peeled and chopped	Lime wedges
Shredded zest and juice 2 small limes	

1 Place all the ingredients except the pork and lime wedges into a blender or food processor and purée until the mixture is almost smooth.

2 Put the pork in a glass baking dish. Pour the coconut mixture over the pork, stirring to make sure the pieces are well coated. Cover and let marinate in the refrigerator about 2 hours, stirring occasionally.

3 Thread the pork cubes onto six skewers and brush with any remaining coconut mixture.

4 Grill over medium heat, turning frequently, for about 12 to 20 minutes. Serve with noodles, and garnished with lime wedges.

Serves 4

Opposite Indonesian pork brochettes

Pork chops with onion and lemongrass stuffing

Grilling these delicious chops gives them a crisp outside to the meat, while the inside stuffing holds the surprise flavor of lemongrass

FOR THE STUFFING

2 large red onions, chopped finely

2 tbsp peanut oil

Pinch chili powder

2 stalks lemongrass, bruised and chopped finely

3 cups fresh bread crumbs

2 big handfuls cilantro, chopped, plus more for garnish

Sea salt and freshly ground black pepper to taste

1 large egg, beaten

4 tbsp unsalted butter, melted

Four 5 to 6 oz pork chops

1 To make the stuffing, preheat the oven to 400°F.

2 Heat the oil in a skillet and cook the onion, chili, and lemongrass for 8 to 10 minutes or until well softened. Remove from the heat and let cool slightly.

3 Mix the bread crumbs with the cilantro, salt, and pepper in a large bowl. Add the onion mixture and blend well. Add the beaten egg, then mix to bind the stuffing. Add a little melted butter if necessary to keep the mixture together.

4 Trim the pork chops of excess fat. Make an incision in each of the chops to create a pocket into which the stuffing can be inserted. Press small balls of stuffing into the pockets.

5 Grill the pork chops over hot heat, 10 minutes per side. Serve topped with a stuffing ball and garnish with chopped cilantro.

Serves 4

Peurco adobo

These will probably be the best pork chops you will ever eat.

Four 1-inch thick pork loin chops

12 oz jar jalapeño peppers, undrained

2 tsp dried oregano

4 cloves garlic, pressed

2 tsp ground cumin

¼ cup cider vinegar

1 Combine all the ingredients except the pork chops in a blender with a steel blade. Purée.

2 Place the chops in a glass dish. Pour the purée over the pork chops and marinate in the refrigerator for 4 hours, or overnight.

3 Grill over medium-hot heat, 5 to 7 minutes per side. Or, cook to the doneness you desire.

Serves 4

Opposite Pork chops with onion and lemongrass stuffing

Guava-glazed baby ribs

Ribs are particularly well suited to fruit-based sauces, and these Caribbean-inspired ribs are no exception.

4 racks baby back pork ribs (1 to 2 lbs each)

¼ tsp ground cloves

⅛ tsp mace

FOR THE ISLAND RUB

¼ cup packed brown sugar

¼ cup sugar

2 tbsp seasoned salt

2 tbsp garlic salt

2 tbsp celery salt

2 tbsp chili powder

2 tbsp freshly ground black pepper

1 tsp allspice

1 tsp ground ginger

½ tsp cayenne pepper

FOR THE GLAZE

1 cup guava paste or fruit purée, such as mango or plum

¼ cup honey

¼ cup fresh orange juice

2 tbsp soy sauce

2 tbsp fresh lime juice

1 tsp ground ginger

½ tsp ground allspice

1 tsp sea salt

½ tsp white pepper

1 Combine the rub ingredients in a medium bowl and blend well. Place in an airtight container and set aside.

2 Combine the glaze ingredients in a small saucepan and cook over medium-low heat, stirring with a whisk. Cook for about 10 minutes until the ingredients have been incorporated. Set aside.

3 Remove the membrane from the back of the ribs. Sprinkle both sides of each rack with the rub. Grill the ribs over medium heat, meat side down, covered, for 4 to 6 hours, turning after 2 hours then again 1 hour later.

4 To test for doneness, take two side-by-side ribs and if they tear apart easily, they are about done. Using a pastry brush, coat each slab on both sides with the glaze, cook for 10 to 15 minutes, then repeat the process.

5 Allow the ribs to rest for 10 to 15 minutes before cutting into pieces to serve.

Serves 8 to 10

Grilled veal chops

This recipe is for all of the "grilling gourmets" out there. It is fantastic with a good Merlot. Panko bread crumbs, which are Japanese, create a crunchier crust than regular bread crumbs and can be purchased in Asian markets.

4 frenched veal chops
    (ask your butcher to do
    this)
2 tbsp garlic salt
2 tsp freshly ground
    black pepper

2 cups panko bread crumbs
½ cup olive oil
1 tbsp minced garlic
8 thin slices prosciutto
4 wedges soft blue-veined
    cheese

1 Season the chops with the garlic salt and pepper.

2 Grill the chops over hot heat, 7 to 9 minutes per side or to the doneness you desire.

3 Combine the bread crumbs, oil, and garlic. Top each chop with two slices of prosciutto and a wedge of cheese. Spoon the bread crumb mixture on top of the cheese. Place on the grill, cover, and cook about 10 minutes or until the cheese melts. Serve hot.

Serves 4

Country-style pork ribs

Ribs are one of the original finger foods, so don't be shy when eating with your hands - grab hold of a rib and take a nice, big bite. Wash it down with some homemade lemonade.

2 lbs pork ribs
¼ cup packed brown sugar
2 tbsp sweet Hungarian
    paprika
1 tbsp sea salt

2 tsp granulated garlic
1 tsp granulated onion
½ tsp ground celery seed
½ tsp cayenne pepper

1 Combine all the ingredients except the ribs in a small bowl and mix well.

2 Trim any excess fat from the ribs and thoroughly season with the rub.

3 Grill the ribs over medium heat, covered, turning every 10 minutes, about 30 to 45 minutes.

Serves 4

Opposite Country-style pork ribs

Grilled carne adovada

The title of this recipe roughly translates to "chile pork." The 24 chiles make it really hot, even without the seeds. It's about the level of heat of Tabasco. The marinade can be made up as a sauce for omelets, which should satisfy most chile heads

2 lbs pork tenderloin

24 dried red chile peppers

2 tbsp bacon fat

2 cups diced onions

4 cloves garlic, minced

2 tbsp all-purpose flour

1 tsp sea salt

½ tsp ground Mexican oregano

1 cup tomato juice

Sour cream and lime wedges, to garnish

1 Wash the chiles and remove the stems and seeds. Place them in a saucepan, cover with water, and boil for 30 minutes. Drain and put the softened chiles through a food mill.

2 Heat the bacon fat in a skillet and sauté the onions and garlic. Add the flour and stir to make a smooth paste. Add the chile pulp, salt, oregano, and tomato juice and simmer, stirring occasionally, for 30 minutes.

3 Slice the tenderloin into ½-inch thick fillets. Place in a glass dish. Marinate in the red chile sauce in the refrigerator overnight.

4 Grill the meat over medium-hot heat, 5 to 7 minutes per side, or until the doneness you desire. Serve with eggs or in a flour tortilla (like a soft taco), garnished with sour cream and lime wedges.

Serves 4

Cuban pork tenderloin with mojo marinade

This is my "uncle" Fidel Castro's favorite meal. Why do I call him my uncle? It's because we share the same birthday!

2 pork tenderloins, trimmed (1½ lbs each)

½ cup fresh orange juice

¼ cup fresh lime juice

8 cloves garlic, minced

1½ tbsp sea salt

1 tbsp ground cumin

1 tbsp ground coriander

1 tbsp sugar

Half a habanero chile, or 1 jalapeño pepper, seeded and chopped finely

1 Combine all the ingredients except the pork in a medium bowl and blend well.

2 Place the tenderloins and the marinade in a resealable plastic bag, seal, and turn to coat. Marinate in the refrigerator for 4 to 6 hours, or overnight.

3 Grill the tenderloins over medium heat, turning every 7 to 10 minutes, for 35 to 45 minutes total. Cook until the internal temperature reaches 145°F to 165°F, being careful not to overcook.

Serves 4 to 6

Opposite Grilled carne adovada

Japanese ginger pork chops

Heat up the sake when these chops are ready to be served. They go well with fried rice or egg noodles.

4 center-cut pork chops

¼ cup soy sauce

2 tbsp shredded gingerroot

2 tbsp mirin (sweet rice wine)

1 Combine all the ingredients except the pork chops and blend well.

2 Place the pork in a glass dish. Pour the mixture over the pork chops and marinate for 2 to 4 hours. Remove from the marinade.

3 Grill over medium-hot heat, 5 to 7 minutes per side, being careful not to overcook and dry out the pork chops.

Serves 4

Curry mango pork chops

No plain-Jane pork chops these. This is a spicy-fruity main dish best served with simple side dishes, such as basmati rice or black beans. A spinach salad will add contrasting color and texture.

Six 1-inch thick center-cut lean pork chops

FOR THE CURRIED MANGO

2 mangoes, cut into bite-sized chunks

2 tbsp unsalted butter, melted

¼ cup packed brown sugar

1 to 1 ½ tsp curry powder

FOR THE PORK CHOPS

1½ tsp shredded gingerroot

3 cloves garlic, pressed

½ cup dry sherry or dry wine

½ cup ginger or orange marmalade

¼ cup soy sauce

2 tbsp light sesame oil

1 To make the curried mango, preheat the oven to 350°F. Place the drained mango in a baking dish or pie plate. Combine the butter, sugar, and curry powder and spoon over the fruit. Bake in the oven for 30 minutes. Set aside and keep warm until needed.

2 For the pork chops, take the point of a knife and make six shallow incisions on each side of the chops. Make a paste with the ginger and garlic and rub it into the meat on both sides, spreading any remaining paste on top of the chops. Set aside.

3 Combine the sherry, marmalade, soy sauce, and sesame oil in a small bowl and mix well. Place the pork chops in a glass dish. Pour the marinade over the pork chops, turning to make sure all sides are coated. Marinate for 30 minutes.

4 Place the chops on the hottest part of the grill and cook, covered, for about 15 minutes, basting occasionally with the marinade and turning 2 or 3 times.

5 Serve, accompanied with the curried mango.

Serves 6

VEGETABLES 6

Feta-stuffed bell peppers

Here is a unique twist on stuffed peppers. If you don't care for anchovies, leave them out, but eliminate the sugar if you do so.

4 red bell peppers, halved and seeded

2 medium tomatoes, quartered

10 oz feta cheese, cut into small cubes

2-oz can anchovies, drained and chopped

1 cup black olives, halved and pitted

8 tsp sugar

Olive oil

16 fresh basil leaves

1 Place a tomato quarter, some cubes of feta, some chopped anchovy, some olive halves, and 1 teaspoon sugar into each pepper half. Drizzle with olive oil and place basil leaves on top.

2 Grill the peppers over medium heat until they are soft and the skin begins to char, about 10 minutes.

Serves 2 to 4

Barbecue-roasted potatoes and onions with olives

These potatoes are a welcome change from the ubiquitous baked potato that seems to be the usual barbecue fare.

1½ lbs potatoes, sliced thinly

2 large onions, sliced thinly

3 tbsp olive oil

1 tbsp white wine vinegar

3 tbsp finely chopped thyme or rosemary

Sea salt and freshly ground black pepper to taste

16 pitted black olives

1 Put the potato and onion into a large bowl. Whisk together the oil and vinegar, and drizzle over the potato mixture. Toss well. Add the thyme, salt, and pepper, and toss again until well coated.

2 Divide the mixture between six large squares of thick foil. Slice the olives into thin rings and scatter them over the top.

3 Close the parcels, being sure to secure the seams. Grill the parcels over medium heat, turning occasionally, about 30 minutes, or until the potatoes are tender.

Serves 6

Opposite Feta-stuffed bell peppers

Grilled Indonesian eggplant

This recipe makes a great vegetarian meal when served with a tossed salad and a crunchy vegetable. As a side dish, it is also a good addition to a meal featuring pork tenderloin.

1 large eggplant, cut into 1/2-inch slices

2 cloves garlic, minced

2 shallots, peeled and chopped finely

1 serrano chile, seeded and chopped finely (use rubber gloves when handling chiles)

1 tbsp toasted sesame oil

1/4 cup crunchy peanut butter

1 tbsp soy sauce

1 tbsp packed light brown sugar

1 tbsp fresh lemon juice

1 cup water

Salt and pepper to taste

1 stick unsalted butter, melted

2 cloves garlic, pressed

1 Lightly sprinkle the eggplant slices with salt, place in a colander, and let drain for about 1 hour. Rinse and pat dry.

2 In a small saucepan, sauté the minced garlic, shallots, and chile in the sesame oil over medium-low heat, stirring occasionally, until the vegetables are soft but not browned. Add the peanut butter and cook, stirring, for 1 minute. Add the soy sauce, brown sugar, lemon juice, and water. Bring to a boil. Reduce until the mixture has slightly thickened. Season to taste with salt and pepper.

3 Combine the melted butter and pressed garlic in a small bowl. Brush the eggplant slices with the garlic butter and grill over medium-hot heat 3 to 4 minutes per side or until done. Transfer to a serving plate and top with the sauce.

Serves 4

Middle Eastern grilled eggplant

This dish of thinly sliced, grilled eggplant is served with a sweet-and-sour pomegranate dressing, a leafy green salad, and fresh, fragrant mint. It is an excellent accompaniment to grilled chicken or lamb. Pomegranate syrup is available in Middle Eastern markets.

1 large eggplant

3 tbsp olive oil

5 cloves garlic, chopped

4 to 5 tbsp pomegranate syrup or molasses

6 tbsp balsamic vinegar

Handful of mixed salad leaves

Sea salt and freshly ground black pepper to taste

3 tbsp finely chopped mint

Pomegranate seeds, to garnish

1 Slice the eggplant, and brush the slices with olive oil.

2 Grill the eggplant slices over a medium heat until they are lightly browned and tender. Remove from the grill and rub with the garlic.

3 Combine the pomegranate syrup with an equal amount of the balsamic vinegar and set aside. Toss the greens with a little oil and the remaining balsamic vinegar, adding salt and pepper as desired.

4 Serve the eggplant slices sprinkled with the pomegranate-vinegar syrup, chopped mint, and pomegranate seeds, with the greens on the side.

Serves 4

Opposite Middle Eastern grilled eggplant

Tofu and tomato kabobs

This dish is delicious when made on a barbecue. For an alternative way of serving, the vegetables and tofu can be nestled in sliced baguettes or wraps.

2 zucchini, cut into thin strips

11 oz firm tofu, cut into ½-inch cubes

24 cherry tomatoes

2 tbsp olive oil

Sea salt and freshly ground black pepper to taste

1 tbsp chopped fresh rosemary

1 tbsp chopped fresh parsley

2 bunches arugula, rinsed

8 metal skewers

FOR THE DRESSING

2 tsp whole-grain mustard

3 tbsp olive oil

2 tbsp balsamic vinegar

2 tsp apple juice

1 Wrap the tofu cubes with the zucchini strips and then thread the tomatoes and wrapped tofu pieces alternately onto the skewers.

2 Brush with olive oil and sprinkle with the salt, pepper, rosemary, and parsley. Grill the kabobs, turning occasionally, for 6 to 8 minutes under a medium heat.

3 For the dressing, mix all the ingredients in a jar and shake well to amalgamate.

4 To serve, lay the arugula on a serving plate, place the kabobs on top, and drizzle with the dressing. Alternatively wrap the dressed kabobs and garnish with parsley.

Serves 4

Penne with grilled eggplant and tomatoes

You can put this dinner together in 15 minutes or less, so you'll have plenty of time to eat and enjoy! Or, try it with zucchini or yellow squash if you're not in the mood for eggplant.

1 large eggplant, cut into ½-inch slices

1 lb tomatoes, each cut in half

Olive oil

Salt and pepper to taste

8 oz penne pasta

¼ cup chopped parsley

2 tbsp olive oil

4 cloves garlic, pressed

¼ cup freshly shredded Parmesan

1 Brush both sides of the eggplant slices and tomato halves with olive oil. Season to taste with salt and pepper. Grill the vegetables over medium heat – the eggplant about 3 to 4 minutes per side or until tender, and the tomatoes until charred, turning occasionally, about 6 to 7 minutes. Let cool.

2 Meanwhile, cook the pasta in a large pot of boiling, salted water until tender but still firm (*al dente*). Drain the pasta and return it to the same pot.

3 Cut the eggplant into strips and the tomatoes into bite-size pieces.

4 Add the eggplant, tomatoes, parsley, olive oil, and garlic to the pasta and toss to blend. Sprinkle with the cheese, season with salt and pepper, and serve immediately.

Serves 4

Opposite Tofu and tomato kabobs

Chili-rice burgers

These burgers can be grilled on the barbecue, but it is a good idea to put them in a grill basket so they can be easily turned over.

3 tbsp olive oil

2 cloves garlic, minced

4 red chiles, seeded and chopped

Heaping ¼ cup short-grain rice

1 large carrot, shredded

2 tbsp tomato paste mixed with 2 tbsp water

2½ cups vegetable stock, plus 1 to 2 tbsp

Sea salt and freshly ground black pepper to taste

1 cup canned kidney beans, drained

½ cup corn kernels

2 tbsp chopped cilantro

1 large tomato, sliced

6 buns, lightly toasted

Chili pepper relish, to serve

1 Heat 2 tablespoons oil in a skillet and sauté the garlic and chile for 5 minutes. Stir in the rice and continue to cook for 3 minutes, stirring occasionally. Stir in the carrot.

2 Add the tomato paste mixture, vegetable stock, salt, and pepper to the skillet. Bring to a boil. Reduce the heat and simmer for 20 minutes, or until the rice is cooked, stirring occasionally and adding a little extra stock if necessary.

3 Add the kidney beans and corn. Cook for another 5 minutes or until the mixture is very stiff and will stick together. Stir in the cilantro and remove from the heat. Let cool.

4 When the mixture is cool enough to handle, wet your hands slightly and shape the mixture into six large burgers. Cover and refrigerate for at least 30 minutes.

5 Brush the burgers with olive oil and grill over medium heat for 4 to 5 minutes, turn carefully, and cook another 3 to 4 minutes or until heated through. To serve, place the burgers on the buns and top with a little chili pepper relish.

Serves 6

Grilled portobello and watercress burgers

Some people think portobellos are the "strip steak" of mushrooms because of their meaty texture. I like to grill them and serve them as an entrée, vegetable, or an accompaniment.

½ cup mayonnaise

1 tbsp Dijon mustard

2 tsp finely chopped rosemary

3 cloves garlic, minced

3 tbsp olive oil

4 large portobello mushrooms, stems trimmed

Salt and pepper to taste

4 whole-wheat buns, toasted

2 bunches watercress

1 Mix the mayonnaise, mustard, rosemary, and 1 minced clove garlic in a bowl and blend well. Cover and refrigerate until needed.

2 Combine the oil and 2 minced cloves garlic in a small bowl and blend well. Thoroughly brush the mushroom caps with the garlic oil and season to taste with salt and pepper. Grill over medium-hot heat 8 to 10 minutes per side, being careful not to let them burn.

3 To serve, spread both sides of the toasted buns with the mayonnaise mixture. Place some watercress on the bottom of the bun, add a mushroom cap, and top with the other slice of the bun.

Serves 4

Opposite Chili-rice burgers

Zucchini with black olives and mint

A simply delicious accompaniment to seafood and fish, this Mediterranean-inspired dish is even good with a burger.

8 black olives, such as kalamata
3 large zucchini, green and yellow varieties
Sea salt and finely ground black pepper
2 tbsp olive oil
3 tbsp coarsely chopped mint
2 tsp fresh lemon juice

1 Pit and thinly slice the olives. Cut the zucchini diagonally into ¼-inch thick slices. Place in a bowl with the salt, pepper, and olive oil. Toss to coat.

2 Grill the zucchini over medium-hot heat until lightly charred and just tender, about 3 to 4 minutes per side. Transfer to a bowl and toss with the olives, mint, and lemon juice.

Serves 4

Zucchini and sweet onion brochettes

The seasoning caramelizes a little during cooking, giving the vegetables a slightly sweet accent, which is totally irresistible.

3 tbsp olive oil
3 tbsp tomato paste
3 tbsp finely chopped fresh rosemary
1 tbsp sugar
24 small onions, peeled
6 zucchini, each cut into 4 pieces
6 metal skewers

1 Combine the oil, tomato paste, rosemary, and sugar in a small bowl and mix well.

2 Put the onions and zucchini in a resealable plastic bag, add the tomato mixture, seal, and turn to coat. Marinate for about 30 minutes.

3 Alternately thread the onions and zucchini onto six metal skewers. Grill over medium-high heat, turning occasionally, until slightly blackened and just cooked through, about 15 minutes.

Serves 6

Squash and apples with brown sugar

Here, wedges of squash and apples are baked in foil, with butter and brown sugar enhancing their natural sweet flavor and luscious texture.

1 small acorn squash
2 tart apples or baking apples
6 tbsp unsalted butter
¼ cup packed light brown sugar
Juice of 1 lemon
Sea salt and ground pepper to taste
Allspice to taste
3 tbsp finely chopped parsley

1 Halve the squash lengthwise. Scoop out and discard the seeds and membranes. Cut each half into 3 wedges.

2 Cut the apples in half and then each half into thirds. Core each wedge.

3 Place the squash and apple wedges on a large sheet of thick foil and top with tablespoons of butter and brown sugar. Sprinkle with the lemon juice, salt, pepper, allspice, and parsley.

4 Close the parcel, being sure to secure the seams. Grill over medium heat, turning the parcel frequently, until the squash is tender, about 40 minutes.

Serves 6

Opposite Zucchini with black olives and mint

Halloumi with brandy and lemon-herb marinade

Grilled halloumi cheese is one of the great pleasures of eating in Cyprus. When cold, halloumi is rubbery, slightly tough, and quite salty; when heated over a grill, it grows soft and supple, imbued with the wonderful smoky scent of the fire. Halloumi can be found in Middle Eastern grocery stores or markets.

2 cups halloumi cheese, cut into ¼-inch slices	Several pinches of *herbes de Provence* or *bouquet garni*
2 tbsp olive oil	1 clove garlic, pressed
2 tbsp brandy	1 lemon, cut in half

1 Combine the cheese with the olive oil, brandy, herbs, garlic, and juice of one lemon half. Marinate for 30 minutes, or up to several hours in the refrigerator.

2 Cut the remaining lemon into wedges and set aside.

3 Grill the halloumi cheese quickly over hot heat, letting it brown lightly on each side, but being careful that it doesn't melt through the rack.

4 Remove the cheese from the hot fire, garnish with the lemon wedges, and serve immediately.

Serves 4

Opposite Halloumi with brandy and lemon-herb marinade

Chinese long beans with cracked black pepper

These beans, also known as yard-long beans, can be found in Asian markets and in some well-stocked supermarkets. They are good with everything from grilled steak and potatoes to fried chicken. Use of a grill basket when grilling the beans would make turning simple.

1 medium red bell pepper	**2 tbsp soy sauce**
2 tbsp olive oil	**1 tbsp water**
1 medium onion, cut into ½-inch slices	**2 tsp sugar**
1 lb Chinese long beans or green beans, trimmed	**1 to 2 tsp cracked black pepper**

1 Rub the bell pepper with olive oil and grill over medium-hot heat, turning, until charred all over. This will take 10 to 15 minutes. Place in a paper bag and set aside.

2 Brush both sides of the onion slices with olive oil and grill until soft and charred, about 4 to 5 minutes per side, or until the doneness you desire. Set aside and keep warm.

3 Combine the soy sauce, water, sugar, and cracked black pepper in a small bowl and blend well.

4 Grill the beans over medium-hot heat, turning as needed, until tender-crisp, 6 to 7 minutes.

5 Place the beans in a serving bowl. Remove the pepper from the bag and peel, discarding the seeds and membranes. Chop and add to the beans. Chop the onions and add to the beans. Pour in the sauce and gently toss. Serve warm.

Serves 4 to 5

Nine-spice grilled vegetables

If you think this seasoning is good with vegetables, try it on your next pork loin. You won't be disappointed.

3 tbsp light brown sugar, dried*

3 tbsp seasoned salt

2 tbsp sweet Hungarian paprika

1 tbsp chili powder

1 tbsp black pepper

2 tsp granulated garlic or garlic powder

1 tsp granulated onion

1 tsp dried basil

1 tsp cayenne

Olive oil

A combination of your favorite vegetables, such as zucchini, yellow squash, bell peppers (red, green, or yellow), onions, mushrooms, potatoes, or sweet potatoes

1 Combine all the ingredients except the olive oil and the vegetables in a small bowl and blend well.

2 Cut all the vegetables into pieces roughly the same size, all about 1/2-inch thick. Brush with the olive oil and sprinkle generously with the spice mixture. Grill over medium-hot heat until just cooked through, turning occasionally – most vegetables will be cooked in about 6 to 7 minutes. Parboil or bake the potatoes and sweet potatoes before grilling for this timetable.

* To make dry brown sugar, spread the sugar out on a cookie sheet and let air-dry for 2 to 3 hours, then sift to break up the clumps.

Makes 1/2 cup spice

Vegetable gyros with tzatziki sauce

Although I'm a proud meat-eater, this is one of my favorite sandwiches – it's healthy and tasty, not to mention filling and satisfying.

FOR THE FILLING

Four 3/4-inch thick slices firm tofu, well drained

1 green bell pepper, seeded and cut into 8 strips

1 red bell pepper, seeded and cut into 8 strips

8 scallions, left whole with green tops trimmed

1/2 cup bottled Italian salad dressing

1/4 cup finely chopped mint

4 pita bread

2 plum tomatoes, sliced thinly

1/2 cup crumbled cheese

FOR THE TZATZIKI SAUCE

1 cup yogurt or sour cream

1/2 cucumber, peeled, seeded and diced

4 cloves garlic, pressed

1/2 tsp sea salt

1/4 tsp white pepper

1 Place the tofu, peppers, and scallions in a glass baking dish. Combine the dressing and mint in a small bowl and mix well. Pour the marinade over the tofu and vegetables, making sure they are well coated. Cover and set aside for 15 minutes.

2 Combine all the tzatziki sauce ingredients in a small bowl and blend well. Cover and refrigerate until needed.

3 Grill the tofu and vegetables over medium heat, basting with the marinade and turning as needed, until lightly charred, about 5 minutes. Remove from the grill and set aside, keeping them warm. Grill the pita bread, turning several times until warm.

4 To assemble the gyro, place the tofu in the middle of the pita bread, and top with a slice of red and green pepper, two scallions, tomato, cheese, and the sauce. Roll up the sandwich and secure with toothpicks. Serve immediately.

Serves 4

Opposite Vegetable gyros with tzatziki sauce

Pesto and mozzarella sub

I love making these sandwiches for picnics - they go nicely with a crisp wine and good company. This recipe makes about $2/3$ cup pesto, which is more than you'll need. Refrigerate the leftovers in an airtight container with a little olive oil poured on top to seal in the color and flavor.

FOR THE PESTO

1 cup fresh basil leaves

3 tbsp walnuts or pine nuts, toasted and chopped

2 cloves garlic, pressed

3 tbsp freshly shredded Parmesan

$1/3$ cup olive oil

Salt and pepper to taste

FOR THE SANDWICH

1 medium onion, cut into $1/2$-inch thick slices

2 bell peppers, red and yellow, quartered and seeded

3 small eggplants, cut into $1/4$-inch thick slices

One 14-inch long Italian bread, cut in half

Olive oil for brushing vegetables and bread

1 cup shredded mozzarella cheese

3 tbsp finely shredded basil leaves, to garnish

1 To make the pesto, combine all the ingredients in a food processor or blender, and blend until smooth. Cover and chill.

2 Brush the onions, peppers, and eggplant with olive oil and grill over medium-hot heat until cooked through, about 4 to 5 minutes per side. Remove the vegetables from the grill and cut the peppers into strips.

3 Brush the cut side of the bread with oil and grill, cut side down, until golden brown and toasted, about 2 to 3 minutes. Spread each piece of bread with 4 tablespoons pesto, and divide the vegetables and cheese between each piece. Wrap the bread in foil and place the parcel back on the grill, until the cheese melts, 3 to 4 minutes. Garnish with the basil leaves, and slice to serve.

Serves 4

Cheese sausages

These tasty treats aren't called sausages because they contain meat, but because of their sausage-like shape. In fact, these cheesy bites are meat-free.

2³/₄ cups fresh bread crumbs

5 oz cheddar cheese, shredded

1 medium onion, chopped

2 tbsp chopped parsley

1 tsp dried mustard

1 tsp Worcestershire sauce

1 tbsp water

Sea salt and freshly ground black pepper to taste

Olive oil

1 Place all the ingredients except the salt, pepper, and oil in a food processor and process until the mixture forms a soft dough. Add the salt and pepper and process a few seconds more.

2 Divide the mixture into eight portions and shape into "sausages."

3 Brush with olive oil and grill over hot heat, turning until browned all over, about 10 minutes.

Serves 2 to 4

Center Pesto and mozzarella sub

Corn on the cob with chipotle butter

Corn on the cob goes with almost every picnic or barbecue dinner, and this corn is no exception. If the chipotle butter is too hot for your palate, try a little garlic butter instead. Make it by combining melted butter and crushed garlic.

1 stick unsalted butter

1½ tbsp canned chipotle chiles in adobo sauce, seeded and finely chopped

1 tbsp fresh lime juice

¼ tsp sea salt

8 ears fresh corn, husked

8 lime wedges

1 Melt the butter in a saucepan over medium heat. Add the chile, lime juice, and salt. Reduce the heat to low and cook for 1 minute, just to blend the flavors. Place the corn on a sheet pan and brush each cob all over with the butter. Cover and refrigerate.

2 Grill the corn over medium-hot heat, turning frequently, cooking until the corn becomes darkened in spots, about 6 to 7 minutes. Serve warm with a lime wedge.

Serves 8

Asparagus spears with saffron aïoli

This vegetable dish is very versatile – it goes with any type of meal, whether it's grilled, barbecued, or roasted. I especially like it with juicy and succulent prime rib.

FOR THE AIOLI

¼ cup red wine vinegar

1 tbsp corn syrup

Large pinch of saffron threads

1 cup mayonnaise

2 to 4 cloves garlic, pressed

Salt and pepper to taste

FOR THE ASPARAGUS

2 lbs asparagus, trimmed

¼ cup olive oil

¼ cup diced red bell pepper

1 Whisk the vinegar, corn syrup, and saffron threads in a saucepan over medium-hot heat. Bring to a boil. Remove from the heat and let cool completely.

2 Mix the mayonnaise and garlic (to taste) in a bowl and blend well. Add the cooled saffron mixture. Season to taste with salt and pepper. Cover and refrigerate until needed.

3 Place the asparagus spears in a glass baking dish. Pour the oil over the asparagus and toss to coat. Grill over medium-hot heat, turning as needed, until tender-crisp, about 4 to 5 minutes. Transfer to a serving platter, garnish with diced red pepper and sea salt. Serve with the aïoli.

Serves 6 to 8

Opposite Asparagus spears with saffron aïoli

Polenta with black bean salsa

This is a hybrid dish, combining Italian polenta with Southwestern Black Bean Salsa. Serve it for lunch or a light dinner, but remember - the polenta must be prepared in advance. Traditional polenta - a coarse grind of cornmeal similar to grits - needs cooking for at least 30 minutes.

6 cups water

2 tsp salt

2 cups polenta

Olive oil

12 oz Cheddar cheese, sliced thinly

1½ cups black bean salsa (see page 144)

1 To make the polenta, lightly oil a loaf pan. Bring the water and salt to a boil in a large saucepan. Slowly add the polenta, stirring constantly and watching for lumps.

2 Reduce the heat to low, and cook, stirring almost constantly, until the polenta forms a thick mass that pulls cleanly away from the sides of the pan, about 30 minutes.

3 Pour the polenta into the loaf pan and smooth the top. Let it cool for at least 30 minutes before turning out.

4 Cut the polenta into slices about 1½-inch thick. To grill, lightly brush the cut edges with the oil. Grill over high heat until the bottom is charred with grill marks, about 3 minutes. Turn the polenta, put a slice of cheese on top, and cook until that side is charred with grill marks, about 3 minutes.

5 Transfer the polenta to a serving plate. Spoon the black bean salsa over the top and serve.

Serves 6

Polenta with corn salad

If you like cornbread, then you're sure to love polenta - think of it as "gourmet cornbread."

FOR THE POLENTA

4 cups water

1 tsp sea salt

1 cup polenta (or yellow cornmeal)

¼ cup shredded Parmesan

Olive oil

FOR THE SALAD

¼ cup olive oil

3 tbsp fresh lime juice

2 cloves garlic, pressed

4 ears fresh corn, husked

1 large red onion, cut into ½-inch thick slices

Olive oil

2½ cups seeded and chopped tomatoes

1 cup cucumber, chopped

¼ cup finely chopped mint

Salt and pepper to taste

1 Bring the water and salt to a boil in a large saucepan. Gradually whisk in the polenta until the mixture is boiling and smooth in texture. Reduce the heat to low. Cook until very thick, whisking often, about 25 minutes (use less time for yellow cornmeal). Whisk in the cheese. Lightly oil an 8 x 8 x 2-inch glass baking dish or metal pan. Spread the mixture in the pan, and cool slightly. Cover and chill at least 6 hours, or overnight.

2 For the salad, whisk the oil, lime juice, and garlic in a small bowl until blended. Cover and set aside.

3 Brush the corn cobs and onion slices with olive oil and grill over medium heat, turning often, until slightly charred and tender - about 8 to 10 minutes for the corn, and 12 to 14 minutes for the onions. Let cool. Cut the kernels off the corn cobs, and chop the onions. Combine the corn and onions with the tomatoes, cucumbers, and mint in a large bowl. Whisk the dressing again and add it to the vegetables. Toss, and season to taste with salt and pepper. Cover and refrigerate.

4 Cut the polenta into four squares, and then cut each square into two triangles. Brush the polenta with olive oil and grill under a medium heat for about 4 to 5 minutes per side. Divide the salad on to plates and serve with the polenta on the side.

Serves 4

SAUCES AND SALSAS

Above left *The* ultimate barbecue sauce **right** Horseradish-mustard cream

The ultimate barbecue sauce

Use this sauce as a glaze if you wish. Brush it over food around the end of the barbecuing process, but take care that it does not burn.

1 tbsp olive oil
1 large onion, chopped finely
3 cloves garlic, chopped finely
1/2 pint stout beer
6 tbsp ketchup
4 tbsp tomato paste
4 tbsp Worcestershire sauce
2 tbsp malt vinegar
2 tbsp packed brown sugar
2 tbsp Dijon mustard
1/2 tsp freshly ground black pepper

1 Heat the oil in a large saucepan and add the onion and garlic. Cook over medium heat, stirring frequently, until the onion is soft but not brown, about 5 minutes.

2 Add the remaining ingredients and stir well.

3 Bring to a boil, cover, and simmer gently, stirring occasionally for 15 to 20 minutes. If the sauce needs thickening, remove the lid and simmer for another 10 minutes until the sauce reaches the desired consistency.

Makes 1 1/2 cups

Horseradish-mustard cream

This sauce is good on all meats and some poultry, particularly beef steak and duck. As a healthier alternative, use yogurt instead of the sour cream.

3 tbsp whole-grain mustard
2 tbsp shredded fresh horseradish or horseradish sauce
1 tsp honey
1 cup sour cream
2 tbsp snipped chives

Mix the mustard and horseradish with the honey. Stir in the sour cream and chives. Refrigerate for at least an hour, then leave at room temperature for 30 minutes before using.

Makes 1 1/4 cups

Molasses barbecue sauce

This barbecue sauce relies on molasses for a thicker, richer, and deeper barbecue flavor. Besides being great with meats, it's also wonderful used to make baked beans.

Generous 1/2 cup molasses
Generous 1/2 cup cider vinegar
Scant 1/2 cup peanut oil
4 tbsp Worcestershire sauce
1/2 tsp Tabasco sauce
1 tbsp paprika
1 tsp chili powder
1 tsp dried mustard
1 crumbled bay leaf
1 tsp garlic powder
1/2 tsp celery salt

Thin the molasses by warming it gently in a medium saucepan. Add the remaining ingredients and mix well.

Makes 1 1/2 cups

Aïoli

Aïoli seems like a gourmet item thanks to its popularity in restaurants, but it's so simple to make, you'll wonder why you haven't done it sooner. It tastes great as a dip not only for grilled items, but for almost anything food, cooked or raw.

1 large egg

1 clove garlic

Juice of ½ lemon

1 tsp dried mustard

Cayenne pepper to taste

1 cup olive oil

1 Blend all the ingredients, except the oil, in a blender or food processor.

2 With the blender running, add the olive oil in a continuous stream until the mixture starts to emulsify. Continue adding the oil in a thin stream until the mixture thickens and all the oil has been used up.

Makes 1¼ cups

Right Aïoli

Salmoriglio

In Sicily, salmoriglio is used as *the* marinade for fish that is to be broiled or grilled, usually threaded onto skewers. Sicilians believe that the only way to make a really good salmoriglio is to add seawater; in the absence of this ingredient, use sea salt.

1 clove garlic

1 tbsp finely chopped parsley

1½ tsp chopped fresh oregano

1 tsp chopped fresh rosemary

¾ cup olive oil, slightly warmed

3 tbsp hot water

4 tbsp fresh lemon juice

Sea salt and freshly ground pepper to taste

1 Put the garlic, herbs, and salt into a mortar or bowl and pound to a paste with pestle or the end of a rolling pin.

2 Pour the oil into a warmed bowl. Using a fork or a whisk, slowly whisk in the hot water followed by the lemon juice until well emulsified. Add the herb and garlic mixture and the salt and pepper.

3 Put the bowl over a saucepan of hot water and warm for 5 minutes, whisking occasionally. Let cool before using.

Makes 1¼ cups

Green chile sauce

This delicious sauce is traditionally made with green New Mexico chiles. However, since they are hard to find year-round, you can substitute mild Anaheim chiles and several jalapeño or serrano chiles to boost the heat. This sauce is a key ingredient in enchiladas, but can also be served with tacos, chops, and many other dishes.

**6 green chiles, plus 3 to 4
jalapeño or serrano chiles**

3 cloves garlic

4 tomatoes, halved

1 onion, peeled and halved

¼ tsp sea salt

1 cup water or chicken broth

1 Grill the chiles, garlic, tomatoes, and onion in a tray directly over the coals until they are brown and blistered. Seed the chiles, and cut them into strips. Peel the garlic. Cut the tomatoes and onions into chunks.

2 Purée all the vegetables with the salt and ½ cup water in a blender or food processor.

3 Put the purée in a medium saucepan with the remaining water and simmer until it reaches the desired consistency. Adjust the seasoning if necessary.

Makes about 2 cups

Asian sweet-and-sour sauce

There are many different recipes for sweet-and-sour sauce. This one is particularly delicious with burgers, chops, and ribs. It is so easy to prepare and can be made quickly, especially if you use canned tomatoes.

1 tbsp olive oil

1 onion sliced thinly

1 clove garlic, minced

**1 green bell pepper, seeded
and sliced thinly**

**One 14-oz can crushed
tomatoes, or 1 lb fresh
tomatoes, skinned and
chopped**

4 tbsp packed brown sugar

1 tsp mixed dried herbs

6 tbsp water

**8-oz can pineapple chunks
in juice**

4 tbsp red wine vinegar

4 tbsp light soy sauce

2 tbsp cornstarch

**Sea salt and freshly ground
pepper to taste**

1 Heat the oil in a saucepan and add the onion, garlic, and pepper. Cook gently, stirring occasionally, until the vegetables are soft but not brown, about 5 minutes.

2 Stir in the tomatoes, sugar, herbs, and water.

3 Drain the pineapple, adding the juice to the saucepan.

4 Whisk together the vinegar, soy sauce, and cornstarch, and add to the sauce.

5 Bring to a boil, stirring, until the sauce thickens and becomes glossy. Reduce heat and simmer gently for 5 minutes.

6 Season with the salt and pepper and add the pineapple chunks. Heat and serve.

Makes about 2 cups

Opposite Green chile sauce

Béarnaise sauce

The tarragon in this sauce provides such a distinctive flavor that you really cannot substitute another herb.

6 sprigs tarragon and chervil, chopped

2 to 3 white peppercorns, crushed

1 tbsp chopped shallot

2 tbsp tarragon vinegar

Generous ¼ cup dry white wine

3 large egg yolks

1 tbsp water

2 sticks unsalted butter, softened

A few drips of lemon juice

Sea salt to taste

Pinch of cayenne pepper

1 Combine half the herbs, the peppercorns, shallots, vinegar, and white wine in a saucepan. Bring to a boil and reduce the mixture to about 2 tablespoons.

2 Beat the egg yolks with the water and add to the reduced liquid. Place in the top of a double boiler containing hot, not boiling, water. Whisk until fluffy.

3 Add the butter, 1 tablespoon at a time, whisking until the sauce has thickened. Season with the lemon juice, salt, and cayenne pepper. Serve warm.

Makes 1 cup

Peppercorn sauce

This is a very pungent green peppercorn sauce. It can be made in advance and reheated just before serving.

1 tsp unsalted butter

1 tbsp peppercorn liquid (from the jar of peppercorns)

1½ tbsp cognac

2 tbsp white wine

2 tbsp canned green peppercorns, drained

1½ cups beef broth

4 tbsp sour cream

1 Combine the butter, peppercorn liquid, cognac, and wine in a saucepan. Bring to a boil, reduce the heat, and simmer until reduced to 1 tablespoon.

2 Add the peppercorns and beef broth and reduce again to about ½ cup.

3 Add the sour cream and salt, bring to a boil, and serve with steaks.

Makes 1½ cups

Onion raita

A refreshing salad to serve with fried dishes, or with grilled steak. It is also a cooking accompaniment to many Indian dishes.

1 onion, sliced finely

2 tbsp vegetable oil

1 tsp cumin seeds

1 red onion, sliced finely

1 small red chile, seeded and chopped finely

2 to 3 tbsp chopped fresh cilantro

1½ cups plain yogurt

Sea salt and freshly ground pepper to taste

1 Heat the oil in a skillet and cook the onion until softened but not browned, 3 to 4 minutes. Add the cumin seeds and cook for another 2 to 3 minutes until golden brown. Transfer to a serving bowl.

2 Add all the remaining ingredients. Allow to stand for 15 minutes before serving, if possible, to allow the flavors to blend.

Makes 2 cups

Above left Peppercorn sauce **right** Onion raita

Mango and red pepper salsa

Spicy fruit salsas are especially good with grilled or broiled fish. Substitute papayas for the mangoes for an equally delicious salsa. For a milder but still somewhat spicy salsa, remove the veins and seeds from the chiles. For a very hot salsa, use one habenero or Scotch bonnet chile (but protect yourself with gloves while handling) instead of one of the jalapeños.

2 ripe mangoes, peeled and diced

1 red bell pepper, seeded and diced

1 to 2 jalapeño or Serrano chiles, finely chopped

2 cloves garlic, chopped

Juice of 1 lime

1/4 to 1/2 red onion, chopped

1/2 cup chopped cilantro

Sea salt to taste

Combine all the ingredients in a medium bowl and mix well. Refrigerate until needed.

Makes 2 cups

Black bean salsa

Black bean salsa is an excellent spicy relish, perfect with fish, chicken, and burgers. To keep it simple, use canned beans, and remember, kidney beans are a good alternative if black beans are hard to find.

16-oz can black beans, or kidney beans, drained and rinsed

1/3 cup chopped red bell pepper

3 scallions, chopped

2 red chiles, chopped finely

3 tbsp chopped cilantro

1 1/2 tsp chopped fresh oregano

1 tbsp olive oil

Juice of 1 lime

Sea salt and freshly ground black pepper

Combine all the ingredients. Let sit for at least 30 minutes for the flavors to develop. Taste, and if necessary adjust the seasoning.

Makes 1 1/2 cups

Salsa cruda

This classic, chunky mixture of chiles and a few flavorings defines Mexican cuisine around the world. As a bonus, it is very healthy as well, and is best made and eaten on the same day.

3 to 5 jalapeño chiles, chopped finely

1 mild green chile

3 scallions (white and green parts), chopped finely

5 cloves garlic, pressed

3 to 5 tomatoes, diced

Pinch of sugar

1/4 tsp cumin, or more to taste

Sea salt to taste

5 to 6 tbsp chopped fresh cilantro

Juice of 1/2 lemon or lime

1 Combine the chiles with the scallions, garlic, and tomato, and then season with the sugar, cumin, and salt.

2 Toss with the cilantro and lemon juice. Add more salt and cumin if necessary. Serve immediately or refrigerate until ready to use.

Makes 3/4 cup

Opposite Mango and red pepper salsa

Onion and chile salsa

Grilling brings out a different side in a chile, as it does with onions and garlic. It mellows these ingredients and draws out their sweetness, giving this salsa a completely different character than those that are made raw.

1 onion, unpeeled, cut in half

10 cloves garlic, whole and unpeeled

3 medium-hot chiles, such as jalapeño, whole

1 green bell pepper, cut in half

Sea salt to taste

Juice of ½ to 1 lemon, or to taste

1 Grill the onion, garlic, chiles, and green pepper over medium-hot heat, covered, turning once, until charred on both sides, 10 to 15 minutes. Remove from the heat and place in a paper bag to cool.

2 When cool enough to handle, remove their skins and stems (remove the seeds from the chiles) and chop. Combine all the ingredients in a medium bowl. Season with the salt and lemon juice.

Makes 1 cup

Mango, papaya, and chile relish

Serve this relish as a side dish with rich barbecued foods, rice, and curries. The mango and papaya must be under-ripe.

2 under-ripe green mangoes, peeled and sliced thinly

1 under-ripe green papaya, peeled and sliced thinly

2 to 3 assorted red chiles,

sliced thinly

Sugar to taste

Sea salt to taste

Serve the sliced mango and papaya sprinkled with half the chiles and let each diner sprinkle the sugar, salt, and additional chiles to his or her taste.

Makes 2 cups

Opposite Mango, papaya, and chile relish

Spicy avocado and red pepper dip

The chili and red bell pepper used in this recipe give a mild taste. For those who enjoy a stronger flavor, adjust accordingly.

1 large avocado, pitted and chopped

1 tsp fresh lemon juice

1 red bell pepper, chopped finely

1 scallion (white and green parts), chopped finely

½ tsp ground coriander

¼ tsp chili powder

2 tbsp plain yogurt

Sea salt and freshly ground pepper to taste

1 Mash the chopped avocado in a small bowl and sprinkle with the lemon juice.

2 Add the remaining ingredients and mix well.

Makes 1½ cups

Hummus

This garbanzo bean dip originates in the Middle East and may be eaten with bread or sliced fresh vegetables.

1 cup garbanzo beans, soaked overnight

2 to 3 cloves garlic

½ cup tahini

⅓ cup olive oil

Sea salt and freshly ground pepper to taste

Juice of ½ lemon (optional)

Paprika

1 Rinse the garbanzo beans under cold running water, then bring them to a boil in a saucepan of fresh water. Simmer for about 1½ hours until tender. Let cool. Drain the beans and reserve some of the water.

2 Purée the beans, garlic, tahini, and oil in a blender or food processor. Add as much reserved water as necessary to make a thick paste - about ⅔ cup. Add salt, pepper, and lemon juice if using.

3 Spoon the hummus into a serving dish and chill. Sprinkle with paprika just before serving.

Makes 1 cup

SALADS AND BREADS 8

Andalusian chopped vegetable salad

When the weather is hot, make up large quantities of this salad and serve it chilled for any and every kind of meal – even breakfast, when it is exquisitely refreshing.

1 large cucumber, diced

3 to 5 small tomatoes, diced

1 carrot, diced

1 red bell pepper, diced

1 green bell pepper, diced (and yellow or orange bell pepper here, if desired)

1 small onion, chopped finely

3 to 5 cloves garlic, pressed

¼ tsp ground cumin or cumin seeds

Sea salt to taste

Juice of 1 lemon

1 tsp sherry vinegar or white wine vinegar

3 tbsp olive oil

Combine the cucumber, tomato, carrot, bell peppers, onion, and garlic in a medium bowl. Toss with the cumin, salt, lemon, sherry vinegar, and oil. Taste for seasoning and chill until ready to eat.

Serves 4

Spiced couscous salad

Couscous should never be boiled. To prepare it, add boiling liquid to the grain, cover it, and let sit until fluffy.

1 small eggplant

1 small green bell pepper

1 small zucchini

2 tbsp olive oil

1 onion, chopped

1 clove garlic, chopped

1 cup uncooked couscous

1 cup boiling chicken broth

1 tbsp toasted pine nuts

1 tbsp fresh cilantro, chopped

Sea salt and freshly ground pepper to taste

1 red onion, thinly sliced, to garnish

1 Trim the eggplant, bell pepper, and zucchini. Cut the vegetables into ½-inch dice, keeping them separate from each other.

2 Heat the oil in a skillet and cook the onion over medium heat until soft and transparent. Add the bell peppers, stir, and cook for 3 minutes. Add the eggplant, stir, and cook for 3 minutes, and then add the zucchini and garlic and cook for another 3 minutes.

3 Stir in the uncooked couscous. Add the boiling chicken broth and bring the mixture back to a boil. Remove from the heat, cover, and let the couscous rest off the heat for 10 minutes.

4 Add the pine nuts, cilantro, salt, and pepper. Serve garnished with thinly sliced red onion.

Serves 4

Opposite Spiced couscous salad

Sweet potato salad

This potato salad uses Indian flavors. If you like, use a mixture of half sweet potatoes and half baking potatoes.

2 medium sweet potatoes, peeled

4 tbsp olive oil

3 tbsp sesame oil

½ tsp cumin seeds

½ tsp coriander seeds

2 red onions, sliced thinly

2 cloves garlic, chopped finely

Juice of 2 limes

1½ cups canned garbanzo beans

4 tbsp chopped cilantro

Sesame seeds, toasted, to garnish

1 Cut the sweet potato into ½-inch dice. Place in a medium saucepan, cover with cold water, and bring to a boil. Cook for 5 minutes. Drain, reserving the cooking liquid.

2 Heat the olive and sesame oils in a skillet over medium-low heat and gently cook the cumin and coriander seeds. Add the sliced onions and cook until they soften and become translucent. Add the garlic and cook for another 2 minutes. Stir in the lime juice, increase the heat to high, and cook for 1 to 2 minutes. Remove from the heat.

3 Gently fold the potatoes and garbanzo beans into the onion mixture, add the cilantro, toss gently, and set aside for at least an hour before serving. Serve sprinkled with toasted sesame seeds as garnish.

Serves 4

Opposite Sweet potato salad

Minted carrot salad

As a substitute for the baby carrots, you may use regular carrots that have been julienned. It will take a little more work to cut them up, but the results will be the same.

1½ lbs baby carrots, washed

3 tbsp olive oil

3 tbsp long-grain rice

About 4 cups chicken broth

Juice of 1 lemon

6 tbsp chopped fresh mint

Sea salt and freshly ground pepper to taste

1 Slice the carrots in half lengthwise. Heat the oil in a deep skillet and cook the carrots over medium-low heat for 4 minutes.

2 Stir in the rice and the broth to cover by about ½-inch. Season with salt and pepper. Cover and simmer until all the liquid has been absorbed and the rice is fluffy.

3 Let cool slightly, then stir in the lemon juice and mint. Chill before serving.

Serves 4

Honey red cabbage

The combination of red cabbage, apples, vinegar, and sugar is not really new, but this recipe includes honey, dill, and garlic for a unique twist.

3 tbsp vegetable oil

1 large onion, sliced thinly

3 cloves garlic, minced

1 medium red cabbage, shredded and chopped

2 tart apples, quartered, cored, and sliced thinly

2 tbsp white wine vinegar

1 tbsp sugar

2 tbsp fresh dill

¼ cup honey

¼ cup sea salt

1 tsp freshly ground black pepper

1 Heat the oil in a large heavy skillet. Add the onion and sauté until soft, about 3 to 4 minutes. Add the garlic and cook another minute. Stir in the cabbage and cook, covered, about 4 minutes or until the cabbage has wilted.

2 Add the apple, vinegar, sugar, and dill. Stir well and continue to cook until the apples are tender, 7 to 8 minutes. Stir in the honey, salt, and pepper, and cook for another 2 minutes.

Serves 6 to 8

Mixed bean salad

A good bean salad needs a tangy dressing to succeed. The garlic and lemon-based dressing provides a tasty complement to the texture of the salad.

1 cup green beans, cut into halves

6 tbsp canned black-eyed peas

4 tbsp canned cannellini beans

4 tbsp canned red kidney beans

1 shallot, sliced

Sea salt and freshly ground pepper to taste

FOR THE DRESSING

½ clove garlic, finely chopped

2 tbsp fresh lemon juice

1 tbsp sugar

4 tbsp chopped fresh parsley

2 medium tomatoes, sliced

A few black olives

1 Cook the green beans in a saucepan of boiling water 3 to 4 minutes. Drain and rinse well.

2 Put all the beans, the shallot, salt, and pepper in a large bowl and mix well.

3 Combine the garlic, lemon juice, sugar, and parsley in a jar and shake well.

4 Lay the sliced tomatoes on a serving plate, pile the bean mixture onto the center, and drizzle with the dressing. Garnish with the olives. Serve with crusty bread.

Serves 4

Opposite Mixed bean salad

Tomato and herb bruschetta

It doesn't matter if these little treats sit for a while once they have been put together. The tomato mixture soaks slightly into the toasted bread, with delightful results.

1½ lbs tomatoes, preferably plum, peeled, seeded, and chopped

2 cloves garlic, finely chopped

Sea salt and freshly ground pepper to taste

1 tbsp balsamic vinegar

1 tbsp olive oil

1 tsp fresh lemon juice

6 slices crusty bread, cut into ½-inch thick slices

4 tbsp chopped fresh basil

1 Put the tomato, garlic, salt, and pepper into a pan. Leave on the side of the grill to gently warm through.

2 Once the tomatoes are warm (not hot), stir in the vinegar, oil, and lemon juice.

3 Toast the bread until golden brown on both sides. Place on to serving plates.

4 Stir the basil into the tomato mixture, pile on top of the bread slices, and serve.

Serves 6

Grilled garlic bread

Everyone who likes garlic, loves garlic bread, so make sure you provide enough. It is a great standby to have on hand for people to enjoy while you are cooking the main course on the barbecue.

1 stick slightly salted butter

3 cloves garlic, pressed

3 tbsp chopped fresh parsley

Freshly ground black pepper

1 French baguette

1 Soften the butter and blend in the garlic, parsley, and some pepper.

2 Cut the bread diagonally into thick slices, cutting nearly but not quite all the way through. Spread the garlic butter on both sides of each slice and reassemble the loaf.

3 Wrap in thick foil and secure the seams. Grill over medium heat, turning occasionally, about 15 minutes until crisp and hot.

Serves 4

Opposite Tomato and herb bruschetta

Stuffed tomatoes

Tapas dishes are often gifts to vegetarians because many contain no meat. This dish is no exception. You can use small or large tomatoes for this recipe, which is a simple and colorful addition to any table.

8 small or 3 large tomatoes

4 hard-cooked eggs, cooled and peeled

3/4 cup aioli (see page 138), or garlic mayonnaise

Salt and freshly ground black pepper to taste

1 tbsp chopped fresh parsley

1 tbsp fresh bread crumbs (for large tomatoes)

Chopped fresh parsley

1 To peel the tomatoes, first cut an X-shaped incision at the top. Cover the tomatoes in boiling water for 10 seconds, and then plunge them into a bowl of ice water for a few seconds. The skins should simply slip off.

2 Take a slice off the tops of the tomatoes, and another slice off the base – just big enough to remove the rounded ends to keep the tomatoes sitting flat on the plate. Reserve the tops if using small tomatoes.

3 Mash the eggs with the mayonnaise, salt, pepper, and parsley.

4 Fill the tomatoes, firmly pressing down the filling. With small tomatoes, replace the lids at a jaunty angle; if using big tomatoes, top with the bread crumbs. Lightly brush the tomatoes with olive oil to prevent them from drying out.

Serves 4

Creole rice

The peppers, corn, and tomatoes make this a colorful rice dish that can brighten up grilled meats.

4 tbsp unsalted butter

2 tbsp olive oil

1 small red onion, chopped finely

1 clove garlic

Scant 1 cup long-grain rice

1 small green bell pepper, diced

15-oz can crushed tomatoes

3 tbsp tomato paste

7-oz can corn kernels

1 small bay leaf

Pinch of cayenne pepper

Sea salt and freshly ground pepper to taste

2 cups chicken broth

2/3 cup dry white wine

1 Heat the butter and oil in a skillet and sauté the onion and garlic until the onion is soft and transparent. Remove the garlic and add the rice, stirring to coat, and continue stirring until the rice is transparent.

2 Stir in the pepper, tomato, tomato paste, corn, bay leaf, cayenne pepper, salt, and pepper.

3 Bring the chicken broth and white wine to a boil in a medium saucepan and pour over the rice. Stir once, cover, and simmer over low heat 10 to 15 minutes. Remove from the heat, take out the bay leaf, and serve.

Serves 4 to 6

Opposite Creole rice

Pasta salad with caramelized onions, olives, and walnuts

Onions are cooked very, very slowly so that they become meltingly sweet and gooey. Then they are simply combined with pasta, black olives, and walnuts, which are added just before serving.

3 tbsp olive oil

2 large onions, sliced very thinly

2 tsp sugar

1½ tbsp tarragon, cider, or white wine vinegar

8 oz pasta, such as penne

4 oz pitted black olives, halved

4 oz walnut halves, lightly toasted and chopped

1 Heat the oil in a large skillet and add the onion and sugar. Cook over low heat, stirring occasionally, until the onions are very soft, sweet, and a rich golden-brown color, 30 to 40 minutes. Let cool about 10 minutes, then stir in the vinegar.

2 Meanwhile, cook the pasta in a large pot of boiling, salted water until tender but still firm (*al dente*). Drain well and transfer to a large bowl. Add the onions, scraping any juices and brown bits from the bottom of the pan. Toss lightly. Cover and let stand until ready to use.

3 Just before serving, gently stir the olives and the walnuts into the pasta. Serve at room temperature.

Serves 6

Fried noodle salad

While this salad isn't exactly low in calories, it features a light dressing that is intensely flavorful. You may omit the omelet if you wish.

8 oz Chinese rice noodles

1 tbsp superfine sugar

1 tbsp light soy sauce

1 tbsp mirin (sweet rice wine)

2 tbsp peanut oil

2 tbsp finely chopped shallots

1 clove garlic, minced

8 oz fresh bean sprouts

1 tbsp fish sauce

2 tbsp fresh lemon juice

6 green chiles, seeded and sliced finely

6 scallions (green and white parts), chopped

3-egg omelet, cooled, and cut into strips

1 bunch cilantro, chopped

1 Cover the noodles with boiling water and let stand 1 minute. Drain and let dry. Combine the sugar, soy sauce, and mirin in a small bowl and set aside.

2 Heat the oil in a deep skillet or wok. Fry the noodles, a little at a time, until golden. Lift them out and drain on paper towels. Gently sauté the shallots and garlic, then drain and set aside with the noodles.

3 Combine the noodles, bean sprouts, fish sauce, lemon juice, chiles, and scallions in a large bowl. Toss well. Garnish with the omelet strips and cilantro.

Serves 4

Opposite Pasta salad with caramelized onions, olives, and walnuts

Classic coleslaw

What barbecue party would be complete without a large bowl of creamy coleslaw? It is easy to make, yet impressive, too. For a change of pace, try replacing half the mayonnaise with yogurt or sour cream.

1 large white cabbage, sliced finely

1 large carrot, shredded

1 large onion, chopped finely

3 tbsp chopped fresh parsley

4 celery stalks, sliced thinly

1 cup mayonnaise

Sea salt and freshly ground pepper to taste

1 Put the cabbage, carrot, onion, parsley, and celery into a large bowl and toss to mix.

2 Season the mayonnaise with salt and pepper and pour into the vegetable mixture. Toss until evenly coated.

3 Cover and chill 2 to 3 hours to allow the flavors to blend. Remove from the refrigerator about 30 minutes before serving. Serve at room temperature.

Serves 8

Gado gado

This traditional Indonesian salad combines raw and cooked vegetables. Here, cubes of tofu are part of the peanut and coconut dressing.

FOR THE PEANUT DRESSING

1 tsp lemongrass purée

1 clove garlic, pressed

1 tsp chili sauce

2 tbsp vegetable oil

1/2 cup crunchy peanut butter

3/4 cup coconut milk

Juice of 1 lime

2 tsp packed brown sugar

2 tsp sweet soy sauce

9 oz firm tofu, cut into small cubes

FOR THE SALAD

1 cup diced sweet potato

2 medium carrots, peeled and sliced thinly

1/2 cup green beans, cut into 1/2-inch lengths

1/2 cucumber, sliced

2 pineapple rings, cut into small pieces

1/2 cup bean sprouts

1/2 cup bok choy, sliced thinly

Chopped red chile

1 For the dressing, place all the dressing ingredients except the tofu in a bowl and beat until smooth. Stir in the tofu and let sit at least one hour.

2 To make the salad, cook the sweet potato and carrot in a pan of boiling water for 5 minutes or until tender. Drain and refresh in cold water. Pat dry with paper towels.

3 Blanch the beans in a pan of boiling water for 1 minute, drain, refresh, and pat dry with paper towels. Mix the cooked vegetables with the cucumber, pineapple pieces, bean sprouts, and shredded bok choy. Pile the vegetable mixture in a serving dish. Spoon the peanut and tofu dressing over the salad, and garnish with the chopped chile.

Serves 4

DESSERTS 9

Nectarines with orange and almond butter

There is something very special about combining nectarines and almonds. The two flavors are a match made in heaven.

3 ripe nectarines

1 large orange

Boiling water

¼ tsp almond extract

½ stick unsalted butter, cut into 6 pieces

1 cup whipped cream or yogurt

6 almond-flavored cookies, crushed

1 Halve the nectarines and remove their pits. Lay each half, cut side up, on a large square of thick foil.

2 Using a vegetable peeler, pare the rind from half the orange and cut the rind into very thin strips. Pour boiling water over the strips and let stand for 10 minutes.

3 In a separate bowl, squeeze the juice from the orange and stir in the almond extract.

4 Into each nectarine half, put some of the orange juice, a piece of butter, and some drained strips of orange rind. Close the foil parcel, being sure to secure the seams.

5 Grill the parcels, seam side up, over medium heat until the fruit has softened slightly and is warmed through, and the butter has melted, about 10 minutes.

6 Open the parcels and top the fruit with whipped cream and the crushed cookies.

Serves 6

Summer fruit packets

Fresh mint adds a wonderful depth of flavor to fruit, especially when the flavor is enhanced with sugar and citrus. Next time you make a fruit salad, add some finely chopped fresh mint for a little extra zing.

2 peaches

Boiling water

½ lb strawberries, hulled and washed

½ lb cherries, pitted

2 Chinese gooseberries (kiwi fruit), peeled and sliced

½ stick unsalted butter

2 tbsp packed brown sugar

Grated rind and juice of 1 orange

4 sprigs fresh mint

1 Place the peaches in a bowl and pour boiling water over them. Let stand 1 minute, then drain and peel. Cut the peaches in half, remove their pits, and slice.

2 Put the strawberries and cherries in a large bowl, and add the sliced peaches and Chinese gooseberries. Gently mix.

3 Cut four large squares of heavy-duty foil. Divide the fruit between the squares.

4 Heat the butter, sugar, orange rind, and orange juice over medium heat in a small saucepan until the sugar has melted. Spoon this mixture over the fruit and top each portion with a sprig of mint. Close the parcels, being sure to secure the seams.

5 Grill the parcels over medium heat for about 10 minutes. Serve with whipped cream or ice cream.

Serves 4

Opposite Nectarines with orange and almond butter

Black bananas with butterscotch sauce

Banana skins are used as natural cooking wrappers in this dessert, and they are served with a uniquely decadent sauce.

½ stick unsalted butter

⅓ cup packed brown sugar

6 tbsp maple syrup

¾ cup heavy cream

½ tsp vanilla extract

4 large bananas

1 Put the butter, brown sugar, and maple syrup in a saucepan and heat slowly over the grill until the butter has just melted. Stir in the cream and vanilla extract. Move to the edge of the barbecue to keep warm.

2 Grill the unpeeled bananas over medium heat, turning once or twice, until black all over, about 15 minutes.

3 Lift the bananas on to a plate. Make a slit along each one, and carefully pull the skin back.

4 Drizzle each banana with some sauce and serve the remainder on the side.

Serves 4

Texas Hill Country peach cobbler

Texas "Hill Country" is famous not only for its barbecue but also for its hot-out-of-the-oven peach cobbler. It is especially good topped with a scoop of homemade vanilla ice cream.

¾ cup all-purpose flour

2 tsp baking powder

1 tsp ground cinnamon

½ tsp allspice

¼ tsp salt

1¾ cup sugar

¾ cup milk

1 tbsp fresh lemon juice

1 stick butter

3 cups sliced fresh peaches

1 Preheat the oven to 350°F. Sift together the flour, baking powder, cinnamon, and allspice. Mix in 1½ cups of the sugar. Slowly stir in the milk and then the lemon juice.

2 Melt the butter in a 9 x 9 x 2-inch baking pan. Pour the batter over the butter, but do not stir. Lay the peaches on top of the batter and sprinkle with the remaining sugar.

3 Bake in the oven for 1 hour or until a toothpick inserted in the center comes out clean. Serve hot or cold.

Serves 6 to 8

Opposite Black bananas with butterscotch sauce

Warm fruit and marshmallow kabobs with chocolate fondue

This is a fun dessert to produce at the end of a barbecue. Everyone dips into the chocolate sauce, and I guarantee there won't be any left over.

16 strawberries, washed and thoroughly dried

Wedge of watermelon, cut into 1½-inch cubes

16 marshmallows

6 oz semisweet chocolate

3 tbsp corn syrup

1 tbsp fresh lemon juice

8 small wooden skewers, soaked

1 Thread the pieces of fruit and marshmallows on to 8 small wooden skewers.

2 Put the chocolate, syrup, and lemon juice in a flameproof dish. Heat gently on the grill, stirring frequently until the mixture is melted, glossy, and smooth. Move to the edge of the grill and keep warm.

3 Cook the kabobs over medium heat for a few minutes, turning once, until just warmed through. The marshmallows will melt very quickly. An alternative is to skewer and grill the marshmallows separately, giving them just a flash over the fire to char.

4 Serve immediately with the chocolate sauce for dipping the kabobs, fondue style.

Serves 4

Center Warm fruit and marshmallow kabobs with chocolate fondue

Hot fruit kabobs with maple cream

If you haven't served kabobs as the main course, now is your chance to conclude the meal with them. You can't lose with this combination of apple, lychees, banana, and fig – it's wonderful!

1¼ cups heavy cream

1 tbsp maple syrup

1 red apple, cored, and cut into 6 wedges

2 bananas, peeled and sliced thickly

12 fresh lychees, peeled and pits removed

3 fresh plump figs, quartered

2 tbsp honey

2 tbsp unsalted butter, melted

6 small metal skewers or bamboo skewers, soaked

1 Put the cream and maple syrup into a bowl and whip lightly to form soft peaks. Cover and chill.

2 Thread the fruit on to six skewers. Stir the honey into the melted butter and brush over the kabobs.

3 Grill the kabobs over medium-high heat, turning frequently and brushing with any remaining honey mixture, until the fruit is slightly scorched and heated through, about 10 minutes.

4 Serve immediately with the maple cream.

Serves 6

Fresh strawberry pie

This was my grandfather's favorite summer dessert. Make it at the peak of the strawberry season, when the strawberries are at their sweetest.

FOR THE CRUST

1 cup all-purpose flour

½ cup margarine

3 tbsp confectioners' sugar

1 tsp vanilla extract

FOR THE FILLING

1 cup water

1 cup sugar

½ tsp salt

3 tbsp cornstarch

½ cup water

3-oz pack strawberry Jell-O

FOR THE TOPPING

2 to 4 cups hulled and halved strawberries

1 cup heavy cream

2 tbsp confectioners' sugar

1 tsp vanilla extract

1 Preheat the oven to 350°F. Make the piecrust by combining the flour, sugar, and vanilla, and cutting in the margarine, until the mixture resembles bread crumbs and forms into a dough. Press the dough into a 9-inch pie pan. Place parchment paper over the shell and cover with pie weights or dried beans. Bake for 15 to 20 minutes until lightly browned. Remove from the oven and cool.

2 For the filling, combine the water, sugar, and salt in a pan. Bring to a boil. Combine the cornstarch and ½ cup water in a small bowl, stirring to make a paste. While constantly stirring, add the paste to the sugar-water mixture. Boil gently until clear and thick. Stir in the Jell-O, remove from the heat, and cool.

3 Arrange the strawberries in the pie shell and carefully pour the cooled mixture over the berries. Chill for several hours.

4 Whip the heavy cream and add the sugar and vanilla. Spoon small dollops of whipped cream around the crust of the pie and serve.

Serves 6 to 8

Watermelon wedges with mango-berry salsa

This is an easy "throw it together" dessert that your friends will ask you to make again and again. It's low in calories yet deliciously sweet.

Twelve 1½-inch thick watermelon wedges

3 cups chopped mango

1 cup fresh strawberries, hulled, and chopped

1 tbsp finely chopped jalapeño chile

¼ cup finely chopped fresh mint

2 tbsp honey

1 Combine all the ingredients except the watermelon in a medium bowl. Refrigerate the salsa and watermelon until chilled.

2 To serve, spoon the mango salsa over the watermelon wedges.

Serves 6 to 12

Opposite Watermelon wedges with mango-berry salsa

Toasted spice cake with warm berries

Use any mix of berries you like in this dessert, or just one if you prefer; it will have a wonderful taste whatever you choose.

1 tsp pumpkin pie spice

1 stick unsalted butter, melted

6 slices of pound cake, each about 1-inch thick

1½ lbs mixed berries, such as blackberries, raspberries, blueberries

2 tbsp apple juice

2 tbsp sugar

2 tbsp Crème de cassis

1 Stir the pumpkin pie spice into the butter and lightly brush it over both sides of the cake slices.

2 Put the berries into a pan with the apple juice and sugar. Cook gently over the grill until the sugar dissolves and the juices begin to run from the fruit. Move the pan to a cool area of the grill and stir in the liqueur.

3 Warm the cake over medium heat, 1 minute per side, or until lightly toasted. The cake will burn easily, so watch it closely.

4 Serve the toasted cake with the warm berries spooned over the top, along with some vanilla ice cream.

Serves 6

Center Toasted spice cake with warm berries

Glazed pears

This dessert was inspired by a classic – pears poached in red wine. In this grill version, a syrup made with red wine is spooned over the pears before they are wrapped in foil and placed on the grill.

6 large, firm pears, peeled, cored, and halved

Grated rind and juice ½ lemon

4 tbsp maple syrup

1 tsp vanilla extract

4 tbsp red wine

3 tbsp chopped pistachios

1 Cut four squares of heavy-duty foil. Lay a pear half on to each square.

2 Combine the remaining ingredients except the pistachios in a small saucepan and heat to boiling. Remove from the heat, and spoon the mixture over each pear. Close the parcels, being sure to secure the seams.

3 Grill the pears over medium heat until they are hot and tender but firm, 5 to 8 minutes.

4 Open each packet and brush or spoon the juices from the packet back over the fruit. Sprinkle a few chopped pistachio nuts over each portion and serve.

Serves 4

Pecan squares

Pecan squares, along with pecan pies, are traditional barbecue fare. These squares are a variation on that theme and will complement all your favorite grilled dishes.

3 sticks unsalted butter, chilled and cut into pieces

½ cup confectioners' sugar

Pinch of salt

2 cups all-purpose flour

1 large egg, beaten

1½ cups packed light brown sugar

¾ cup dark corn syrup

1½ tbsp vanilla extract

4 cups pecan halves

1 Preheat the oven to 375°F.

2 Combine half the butter, the confectioners' sugar, and salt in a food processor. Process until you begin to see moist clumps. Add the flour and beaten egg and process just until a dough forms.

3 Press the dough into the bottom, and about ¾-inch up the sides, of a 9 x 13 x 2-inch baking pan. Bake until the crust is golden brown, about 20 to 25 minutes. Remove and cool slightly, but do not turn off the oven.

4 Bring the remaining half of the butter, brown sugar, and corn syrup to a boil in a heavy saucepan, stirring frequently. Boil for 2 minutes. Add the vanilla and stir in the pecans. Remove from the heat and pour the pecan mixture into the prepared crust. Bake until the filling sets and bubbles, about 25 minutes. Remove and cool completely on a wire rack. To serve, cut into 2-inch squares.

Makes about 24

Fluffy nutters

This dessert is a real kid pleaser, and the adults will love it, too.

18-oz jar peanut butter, plain or crunchy

7½-oz jar Marshmallow Fluff

Ten 9-inch flour tortillas

1 Thinly spread peanut butter over one tortilla to about ½-inch from the edges, and do the same on another tortilla with the Marshmallow Fluff. Put the two tortillas together like a sandwich (filling to filling).

2 Grill over medium heat for 1 to 3 minutes per side, until it is heated through and melts together. Cut into pie-shaped triangles and serve.

Makes about 15

Index